Dear Michelle,

Dear Michelle,

Letters from an Old Friend in a New Life

Samuel Gerard

A collection of creative correspondences

A PEACE CORPS WRITERS BOOK
2022

DEAR MICHELLE,
LETTERS FROM AN OLD FRIEND IN A NEW LIFE

A Peace Corps Writers Book — an imprint of Peace Corps
Worldwide

Printed in the United States of America
by Peace Corps Writers of Oakland, California.

This is a work of creative nonfiction. Some parts have been
fictionalized in varying degrees, for various purposes.

For more information, contact
peacecorpsworldwide@gmail.com.
Peace Corps Writers and the Peace Corps Writers colophon
are trademarks of PeaceCorpsWorldwide.org.

ISBN-13: 978-1-950444-45-8
Library of Congress Control Number: 2022911274
First Peace Corps Writers Edition, April 2022

For all those to whom these letters may have been addressed

Table of Contents

Dear Michelle,

1.

"Man is a mystery. It needs to be unraveled, and if you spend your whole life unravelling it, don't say that you've wasted time. I am studying that mystery because I want to be a human being."

Fyodor Dostoyevsky

Dear Michelle,

I feel I must start this all with an apology, even if you always told me I should be saying "sorry" less.

I was wrong to keep from writing for as long as I have, especially when I promised at the onset of our separation that I would share this experience with you. I assured you I would, as often as I could, keep alive the story alive, one that we began together, through texts, phone calls, and most importantly for their ability to capture the depth of human experience, letters.

Perhaps it took me until now to understand what that story is, that these experiences disguised within everyday life are exactly what I pledged to tell you about when I said goodbye, dreaming a tangible dream of a distant land and epochal adventure.

I wish I could say my absence from your mailbox is because I finally discovered what was worth sharing.

More truthfully, and to my greater regret, this is not why you have waited months to read these words. I've thought back to those first months often, and I have nearly as many opening lines of various letters in my notes as I do themes and motifs and clips of dialogue for stories I hope to write while I'm here (the core of me being aware that most of either will forever be nothing more than promising premises). The more I sought an excuse, the more those unwritten papers piled in my mind, until I was forced to face their frailty as they were all swept away by the truth. Though the plainer the explanation the less I deemed it worthy of reestablishing our communication, I was left with a simple realization, and this was the only one I had left.

For a while I was, simply, swept away in the whirlwind. All that was new. My silence was nothing more.

It seems a poor explanation even as I write and reread it, as I hold the preceding paragraph in context. I am horrified by its simplicity, especially considering the lengths I have often gone to explain away my faults, be these justifications presented to you, my mom, my childhood friends, or my employer. Fitting rationalizations are a large part of what got me here, and yet I sit here bereft of any.

I did not write to you because I was lost in my new life. That is all. Though, to tell the full story, I internalized this tumult rather than relate the journey to another, to you, and thereby, entertaining the possibility of processing or understanding anything at all. I did not write because I did not want to process; you did not hear from me because I did not want to understand. I said goodbye to us, to my comfort, and so many other things when I came here, and I was scared to look back, because to do so would be to regard myself in my entirety, to reconnect with the person I came here to hide from. I could not bring myself to look because I knew I couldn't change him. Removed from where I had been, I saw a clear past from where I was, and was ashamed of my life. Not the life I had chosen to live, as I had existed largely at the whims of my circumstantial currents. Yet this will of course be lost on you. What I can say, and what I hope you can relate to, as I sit in this threadbare room in my own forgotten corner of the world and wonder if the stars are out tonight (I don't have the gall to check and risk an interaction with my host mother) I know now that a change of scenery does not mean a change of heart.

I'm sorry, Michelle.

Initially, during our time apart I was intent on discovering the intricacies of my own personality, subtle intention within my more apparent motivations of escape, adventure, and time, and isolation has allowed this desire permanent occupancy in the forefront of my waking and sleeping mind. Never have I spent such time alone, and at the complete mercy of my inner self, a latent guest no longer. Do you remember the excitement with which I spoke to you of the awakening of my own awareness? I was ignorant then of solitude, and as such it has led me on a path of internal revelation unlike any I anticipated or welcomed. The more I learned of my consciousness the more I turned away the mind's eye, scared to uncover the patterns of thought and behavior which led me to the plaguing vices which I sought to rid myself of by external change. I began to grudgingly unearth myself, as much by happenstance as a willing desire to do so, brought about by night after night at an empty table with the dinner's chosen clatter a cursory distraction from the reflection in my computer who faced me when the YouTube video ended.

The accidental self-discovery (I hope you can forgive the cliché; I cannot word it differently or better despite how rudimentary it feels to type the words self and discovery in such proximity) I'm describing, or, at least, attempting to, showed me a person who was lost. Someone who had existed in almost his entirety at the whim of circumstance. I retreated from this self. Myself.

Slowly, however, excitement infiltrated fear. While at the outset I was wary of this knowledge of my being, as I can most descriptively put it, I came to understand its virtues because I recognized the habits of my past in the mistakes I made in the present. In contrast to before, and, in turn, most consequentially, I now had an outline which finally made sense of the life I had lived to this moment. It was terrifying, to be so aware of what keeps me staring at the ceiling while Bob Ross paints a second and third picture which will not coax the night's dreams, but I also knew at last how to make real the goals I have carried and been discouraged from for so long. Of course my good faith and devotion to self-betterment has always failed!

How could I seek to improve someone I did not know? I was applying coats of paint in the dark, trying to color my soul without ever seeing the canvas underneath. As such, previous attempts to rectify myself with the person I wanted to be were bound to be superficial. They were as brief as the memory of the quote or event which inspired them. No wonder any of my previous attempts, crying in my car on a tired night in Tallahassee or pining over and sharing in the emotions of the scripted development of characters my angsty heart felt most deeply related to, led to a bitter lack of any tangible transformation!

However, now that I see me, or at least, have begun to, I know what I might do to achieve the self I have wished, at each of these moments of reflection, to be. It is the self who caused those tears, who was embodied just enough in those fictions to capture the underdeveloped persona I was and hold me in the subtle potential of more, of healthier, of better.

Naturally, this dualistic discovery has led to an ever-more furious consumption of that which might define the Sam being striven towards. You have known me long enough to be privy to the crippling anxiety of choice which faces every decision I have ever made. Remember when I balked at the cheese platter the old waiter served us at that hidden gem of a restaurant next to the mattress store? And how I told you how many outfit changes I always made before our dates, which you didn't believe until you saw it for yourself? This indecision has never been unique to cheeses and t-shirts, and presently, within this formative experience, applies to the building blocks which will make up the person who emerges from this time abroad.

The years spent far from all that is familiar or permanent, from you, seem to me like the preparation for a presentation, whereby, at the culmination of my service that I have dedicated to finding myself, I will return to the life I left, to you, and display whom I have found. Who I have become or stayed as. I am writing the new play by which I will be judged, every word meticulously chosen and second, third, and fourth-guessed. This new script is comprised by my beliefs, my motivations, my moral code, my life goals, my essence, my motivations, my purpose. I am simultaneously an actor, stepping behind the curtains and away from the displeased audience, memorizing these new lines given him and are promised to be welcomed and applauded. The tension thus lent to the end of these two years, that they might yield the final product of my being, a new and complete self, leads me to voraciously consider every passing desire for who that person might be. I, therefore, struggled, and continue to consume and embody concepts far too complex for the passing thoughts I regard them with, for it is all the time I have.

I might, for example, read an article about existentialism and be convinced it is the philosophy that will define the philosophical aspect of my homecoming. Yet, after hours spent studying the subject, I am dismayed at how little I remember. And if I am further disheartened by the failure of my rehearsals to incorporate the philosophy into my thought, behavior, or, most importantly, conversations, trial interactions of my developing persona with other human beings, what then can I expect at the culmination? How can I change if I cannot digest any of the information which will enable it? So, after another failure, I return to my small apartment and disappear into a different and adjusted informational binge, when a melancholic movie suggests I ought to learn French. What a unique characteristic that would be! And just as I did before, I am consumed by the fresh and untried only if they remain so. Once a goal spurns a first and desultory attempt at incorporation, as any true progress surely will, I am very hard-pressed to seek it further. The volatile way in which I select my improvements has guaranteed I make none.

But it seems I now have time, and in this time, I have discovered what some may call a framework, a chance, a foundation for concrete improvement. In the silence, in the solitude, I have come to know Sam better than ever before, and even by writing this letter I begin to see the components of sustainable self-improvement more clearly. I am excited by the prospect, and motivated to hold myself accountable to these in the future.

Still (and lastly, I swear), I wonder if this mindset is the reason I feel so often disconnected from my daily experience of this new life in Ukraine, as all of this is but rehearsal for my return to "true" existence. While I detach from the previously unbeknownst or unchangeable way of being which has always defined my upbringing from the moment it became an independent endeavor,

I find that I have also detached myself from the experience of the interim. The scenes which play out before my eyes are the scenes of a movie I glance at from deep inside my psyche, my consciousness preoccupied in an endless pacing through the space between my ears, and no amount of stark originality between these moments can bring me into them fully. My hope is, that by the time my crisis of identity and the angst by which it is fueled succumb to the selfish attention I give them, when I determine that which lays behind the eyes of my man in the mirror, I might be able to actively participate in what they see. Until then, I write these memories as one who saw them in a dream, one with sufficient detail to blur the recollection of reality, that they might be preserved and appreciated for what they were once I am solved enough to face them.

With these rambling thoughts, along with a myriad of undefined others, keeping sleep at bay, I renew my promise to you, Michelle. I rub my red eyes and I stare at this page and I tell myself I will tell you my story.

Whether this proves to be a cohesive narrative, a hero's journey with a conclusion befitting its discernable moral, or a mere collection of moments, incoherent, unresolved, waiting to be forgotten, to be replaced by in time, is unknowable, as stories can only truly written once their ending is clear. Writing while I live it risks endlessness, the futility of forever, where no memory is more meaningful than the next because there will always be another. It risks purpose, as well, either prematurely applied or lost in the continual adaptation of linear life unceasing. And yet, I cannot keep waiting to write to you, because I cannot keep you waiting. I promised to tell you about my life, either self-contained or unsettled, so I risk what may be more satisfying for what may be what I owe you. I remember what you told me, as we sat crying with each other, desperate to prolong the late hours of our last night, that my life is not a novel, and hope you'll forgive me for taking this to heart, and presenting my life as it is, not as it might, or ought to, be.

Whether this endeavor, the construction of this story, if that is what it becomes, as it happens, or the transcription these moments as their own that remain distinct, whether this proves to be for your benefit, for mine, or for both our sakes, I eagerly embark upon their retelling for what it may make up for, and what it may build. I am grateful for this chance to communicate myself to you, through thought and memory, through what I've already lived and what I mean to, through letters like chapters. Be it to discover a meaning within them, a purpose in itself, or lend them meaning by their sharing, their purpose for you.

I hope, however, more than anything irreal, more than these greater, personally inconsequential themes, you might forgive me for making you wait so long to be, to remain, and to know that you are, a part of my life.

I hope, as well, you will tell me yours.

Determined,

Sam

2.

"He who binds himself to a joy does the winged life destroy;
But he who kisses the joy as it flies lives in eternity's sunrise"

William Blake

Dear Michelle,

I know it's been a while.

I hope you're doing well. Or I hope you're hanging in there. Or I hope you're happy. Or whatever I could say to ensure you'd know I meant it, that you'd recognize the words weren't a hope, auto-filled.

After my last letter, I imagine a part of you is wondering, likely worrying, over the extent to which the following paragraphs will contain news about my life here, rather than a fresh self-exposition of my psyche. It's a valid concern.

The problem with letters is that no one writes them with you. You're not hear to listen, to guide me to what I really mean for you to hear. Instead, I latch onto a thought, and the pen follows.

There's no one to put their hand against my chest, to push me up when I begin to fall into myself.

It's so easy to fall.

With a blank page and the only goal to illuminate my inner experience, there will always be a danger these letters become more akin to journal entries, esoteric and mired.

In my last letter, the first I actually sent, for example, I wrote all at once what I had never could before, what I could only after I'd left. Rather than a story, I spewed sentiments whose words were empty and whose guilt was no longer needed, as was the person they portrayed.

I wanted to tell you so many other things. I wanted to give you, from the outset, the stories I'd promised. I wanted to ask about you. I wanted to keep it light; you deserved as much. Yet, when I penned "Dear Michelle," it was as if I'd pricked my heart with your name, tempting emotion to dispel the doubts which sent every other attempt in the direction of my trash. These inhibitions dammed any narrative. I realized, upon several fruitless, frustrating attempts to avoid this levee, a block I had mistaken for the one inherent to writing, I could only say what I ought to have.

What gushed forth, then, swept away all thought of the blinking cursor. Through that tiny breach, two words, a quintessential beginning and your first name, so much of my soul spilled I was unable to keep it in check. What I'd successfully suppressed to even think of you at all gratefully gushed forth.

When it was over, I felt a peace of mind unrecognized since I had begun to hastily explore it between the spells of intoxicating insanity that are my norm abroad. As such, it felt a disservice to alter its effusions.

I did not, at the time, consider the effects of such a confession, one you long deserved and must have once wished to hear, on you, when you read it.

I have, since, and understand how unfair it was to abuse this medium of communication to relieve myself of the weight of our context, while it was impossible for you to immediately reply or contend.

Thus, rather than wait for your reply, I hope you will forgive my intrusive apprehensions and allow me to redeem the intent of these letters with a story. I hope it will make for lighter reading, and give you enough to respond to.

The rest, I am sure, will be a conversation for a later day, if at all. My guilt is mine to carry, not yours to forgive me from.

As the postmarked date suggests, it took me some time to find this letter. After inundating you with myself, I wanted to write you a more complete depiction of my life here, and by encompassing more of the world around me, avert further self-indulgence and

11

perhaps even parlay the damage I may have caused with my last communication. I regret that the result is hardly more than a very private publishing of my diary, but I believe there is enough of a setting to offset a persistent narrator.

After such a drastic change in life's circumstances, I had a lot of inhibitions about where to find the stories worth telling. When everything is new, it seems as if everything is worthy of being a story, though the mass of life is a regular and deeply personal affair, no matter where it is spent. I wanted to share it all and settled for sharing nothing. I wanted to perfectly encapsulate what my new life has been and is like, while simultaneously write something exciting enough to justify the burden of my departure to come in search of it. So expectation stifled experience, as it often does, until I went on a walk. When the steady plodding of my feet eventually overcame the course I plotted, circumstance wrested control of my mind, and life insisted its variableness.

It was a pleasantly peaceful afternoon in the early Ukrainian fall. The sun was a good hot, the way a stifling car warms you after spending too much of the day in an overly conditioned room. The stillness of the day's intermittent hours was in full effect, time allotted for the day's errands, our language training had concluded, and an hour remained before the city's employed returned home to its outskirts. The children were playing in our tutor's apartment enclave, a patchy square block whose rusty swings were painted in vibrant colors and the grass and weeds grew bright green around the home gardens and inadvertent footpaths. They threw some crabapples over our heads, and we chased them away, laughing because we did not speak each other's language.

At the bus stop, I parted ways with my language group, the 5 individuals our program essentially demanded I be around at all times. I had a progress assessment meeting with our tutor in an hour, and I knew the busses did come quickly enough to bring me home and back in time. I said goodbye in a low tone, still extremely reticent to use English in public, especially in or around transportation. We were the only ones in the city who ever spoke it, and the attention it garnered embarrassed me.

Then, I went for a walk.

Across from the stop, with its perpetually-closed coffee shop, were a series of wooden stands, much like the storage sheds you and I might be accustomed to seeing in a midwestern uncle's backyard. Rather than rusting lawn care equipment, however, these were inhabited. Each had a sliding glass window display, in which were perched the products these hermit-esque merchants had collected and spent their days sitting behind. On the brightest days it was impossible to tell if there really was a person behind the unrefrigerated cheeses, the second-hand bread, the homegrown persimmons, the other various artisan produce and thin cigarettes, but behind the reflection was always, surely, an attendant. Even after I realized these huts were the only place to buy decent fruit, I avoided them in my early weeks here. Despite the convenience, the direct opportunity to support local growers, and the long lines each of them inexplicably boasted, though we were on the outskirts of the city proper and the line of five all sold the same within meters of another, none of their merchandise had barcodes. Far from comfortable with my grasp of the vocabulary for buying and selling and food and money, I much preferred the tired shops, where at least my total would be digitally displayed. So today, much like every afternoon, I walked astride the stands, sentinels awaiting my refutation of my constraining self-awareness, along the dirt pathway which led to a small grocery store on the first floor of a very Soviet-era apartment building.

They were all Soviet-era apartment buildings. The one I called home, the ones which sheltered the courtyard well where we drew our water, the one where I played soccer with kids whose curious mothers watched from their windowsills. This particular façade was unique in its first floor storefront, with its Cyrillic letters and 80's inspired marketing posters which made the structure all the more brutal. Brutal as in brutalism, an architectural style I could best describe by encouraging you to google the word. Whether thanks to my host grandmother, Nina, and the warmth of her home on the second floor, where kefir coagulated on the balcony, or the collective impression and familiarity of this city, these cookie-cutter blocs were becoming charming.

Even if the pale green numbers above the register, for the same drinkable yogurt stands 3 and 5 also sold, were higher than the totals voiced to me by a family vendor, the process and product under the stale fluorescents was more convenient and colder, respectively.

I stood outside the store and drank my purchase straightaway, imitating a few locals I thought had been especially emblematic of their customs. I was careful to avoid eye contact with the group of young men who piled out clown-car-like from a van marked with a peeling logo whose lightning bolt signified some kind of electrical service.

Bolstered by the sugar I had mistaken for protein on the nutrition label, I set off with a purposeful pace towards the church on top of the hill. Usually, I wandered slowly, and with less intention, but I had a destination, and a time limit.

In the distance was a the tall and sky blue church. Its steeple stood prominent on the nearby summit, a single hill which denoted the horizon and sheltered the flatlands beyond. The slender belfry seemed a stark contrast to the apartment buildings, juxtaposed and rising defiantly resolute against their plain skyline at the extremity of the planned development, a symbol of the urban landscape's limitations in a country where familial agricultural still thrived, a beacon of the quaint and supposedly-former way of life which still thrived outside the city's strict extremities, where the urban landscape finally, fully, and rapidly gave way to farmland. On the first bus into Zhytomyr, I remember the initial blending of homestead and high rise had made it impossible to tell which custom was encroaching on the other.

This sanctified marker, then, bathed in the morning's pensive light or the evening's somber sun, had caught my eye twice a day for weeks, dominating a scene that daily greeted and dismissed me as I disembarked or boarded the marshrutka on my way to and from my tutor's apartment.

In routine, the church remained noticeable. I was, therefore, determined to discover it for myself.

To reach its hill, I had to leave the main street. The gravel throughway, I was told, wound slowly out of town and soon lost its sidewalk. With a thought for the normative style of driving here and that walking on the road itself was akin to suicide, and considering my coming appointment, I spotted an opening in the thicket with what appeared a more direct route. Ducking under some bramble, I found a worn trail, bordered by old trees and blooming bushes, littered with snack wrappings and bottles and intermittent private gardens, with chickens and wire fencing and matrons and their curious stares and hands full of nearly-complete tasks.

I stepped into the countryside.

On this footpath, shared then only by the more independent livestock and a few individuals for whom the work day had ended early, I felt myself privy to a vastly different space than the Ukraine I had encountered.

The familiar grey and crumbling buildings were replaced by quaint homesteads, beautiful in their color and chaos, with gaudy iron gates, kaleidoscopic walls, and overgrown vegetation. The natural elements of their setting: the shade, the woods, the sounds of the nearby creek, lent the locale an ethereal energy. With birds whimsically chasing each other overhead, their flitting calls familiar in any language, and the murmur of residents going about their days, an ambient noise equally comforting despite the foreign backdrop, I was transported, and glided gleefully along the afternoon.

The trampled grass, my heart lightened by the bright day and the sense of comfort available in anywhere in nature, brought me to a stream. The tall, underwater moss gave the shallow depths a luminous green, despite the deep crystal sky above it was supposed to reflect. Saddling the current was a pedestrian bridge, wide enough for a single person and looking to have been crossed by more than its fair share. The design, in keeping with the theme surrounding, looked as though it had been fashioned by some enterprising locals who wanted the shortest distance between work and home and were not quite held to the same standards as professional pedestrian bridge builders. Like much of the preserved aspects of this country, the crossing was workable, its function was to function, and it would continue to do so for more years than I've been around or will be around for, so long as it remains undisturbed. Aesthetics and safety guidelines are an afterthought, a privilege of those with the time to consider them.

Strangely, though, and I pause here, only to say that the more time I spend with the simple solutions the more I question our obsession with superficial considerations. If a bridge is more than a couple of hastily-welded sheets of rusted metal with two matching rails alongside, if a crossing has been verified by a certified inspector instead of a thousand successful crossings, is it truly any better a means by which people move from one point to another? With all our care and attention, our bridges will still break. Why shouldn't we take a more practical approach, then? Does development have such diminishing returns that our current state of affairs is antithetical to efficiency? Take a ride in any public transportation here, and you'll understand the utilitarian mindset I describe. Compare timetables, crash statistics, and user reviews, and you'll wonder why we spend so much on public transportation that yields the same result as an outfitted school bus whose driver only accepts cash, which he will stuff in the glove box decorated with icons of the virgin Mary and Shaktar Donetsk stickers.

This critique of American over-exceptionalism lost some salience when, after waiting for a man and his one-speed bicycle (similarly, out of practicality, not a trend towards fixed gears) to cross, I actually stepped out over the water. Halfway across I had completely abandoned the thought, and would've given anything for a sounder footing, staring down an afternoon-spoiling plunge from these rickety, rotten boards.

Nevertheless, when I reached the other side as dry as I would've had this bridge been made of cement or within the last decade, I recovered that notion. Are we really better off for the efforts we make towards impractical progress? Should bridges be assessed by the confidence they inspire as well as their effectiveness at transporting their wares across the chasms they span? If so, what is the value of this assurance, and is it worth the disparity between our infrastructure expenditures?

Please know these considerations are rhetorical. I include them, and likely will many more, to substantiate my inner monologue and demonstrate the trivialities of what the displaced mind is concerned with when facing a world entirely outside its own. Whether they read as critical or inconsequential is a matter I avoid by handwriting these and making revision impractical, though I expect they afford some measure of intimacy unavailable to a better streamlined story.

Besides, when have I ever told you just the facts.

That sparse, encroaching forest continued on the far bank. The decorative fencing, the upkept homesteads and their tended gardens, the residents striding purposefully from one place to another, those last bastions of an urban, at least structured, lifestyle, did not. There were still fences and homes and flowers, but nature's perpetual reclamation was evident in their disorder and rust and wild. There were people, as well, but their eyes met mine and lingered, and their smiles and pace of work or walk betrayed an aimlessness available to those for whom tasks are unceasing, for whom destinations are uncertain. A stream's-width further from the city, and I had discovered the countryside.

Like a young metropolitan orphan in a turn-of-the-century novel, I marveled at the wistfulness, perfectly preserved despite my ignorance of this way of life. The stream bubbled more noisily, crickets chirped in the sunlight, and the clouds arrested movement. A few chickens clucked at me from behind the curtain of a magnificent willow tree, roaming the ravines before they were collected at sunset. An intrepid goose who shared the footpath squawked a warning, and bade me give a wide berth as I passed. I stood aside, and noticed an old woman, standing still on a fairytale porch, clutching a handmade broom and looking strangely at the stranger overdressed for the occasion of materializing out of the woods and into her yard. I smiled, and nodded, and remembered neither were the usual Ukrainian passing interactions. Her blank stare continued, and told me as much. So, instead, I smiled at myself, took a deep breath of her place, and started up for the church.

This path, as you may well imagine in such a devout country, was the most pronounced of any I'd encountered since I'd turned off from the asphalt. I climbed what was surely a bustling route on Sunday mornings, and wondered how the local elderly did so with such routine.

At the top of the hill was another wrought-iron fence. This, as well as its many religious symbols, was distinct from the others in its effect: this was much more ornate, more effective, and in far worse shape than its domestic counterparts. Beyond, I recognized the structed I'd seen from the valley bus stop below, and that it's gate, complete with an ironically modern padlock, protected what was previously a place of worship and currently a nesting-ground for local rodents. The chapel, like so many other buildings I had seen, was abandoned. The well-trodden path continued further, and likely led to the church in use, but I had not come to pray.

The blue façade was worth coming to see all the more for its emptiness.

I climbed into the courtyard, oblivious to my attire, and colored my grass-stained khakis with the brown of stale, flaking iron. The church, an object of adventure where so often, to this point, I'd had none, was set in a scene so satisfyingly fantastical I felt I needed to immerse myself within it to have any hope of remembering the afternoon as more than a dream.

Springing from the gate's arch I landed on bright green grass, long and mercifully disguising any plump summer slugs which may have lent their lives to my soft landing. I brushed my knees and made sure my bag was secure, then set off for the courtyard.

Everywhere were signs of deterioration and of growth, one of thousands of testimonies to entropy's ultimate triumph sprinkled across this ancient country. Overgrowth spilled through the peeling pickets, holding the remains of parish gardens. Below the weeds, a few blossoming trees fought a silent and slow and invisible territory war, their branches colorful, their leaves bright and peacefully swaying in the soft wind. Noisy spheres of gnats hovered indiscriminately. After I encountered a few I wanted to be annoyed, but without their signs of life the locale might well have been haunting, and so I was grateful for their low hum and the wildflowers which offset the granite gravestones still visible amidst the pasture. The few which still held words I could not read. If my grasp of Ukrainian had been better than tentative I might've spotted that were written in Russian, and faded beyond legibility.

To my right, among more forgotten tombstones, was this forgotten place's memorial to the great war which had touched even it. A soldier, spray-painted in a once-lustrous silver, knelt atop a block of black marble and forever laid a wreath of fake flowers on the grave of a comrade, or, if not forever, for as long as his metal knee remained smelted to the stone, or the paper garland was grasped by his tragic hand. These wreaths of brightly-colored plastic blooms were the kind I'd become familiar with, their neon colors were easy to spot against the gravestones and Orthodox crosses they adorned and dotted (I later learned they were a hallmark of an annual tradition, when relatives and descendants spent the morning of November 1st in their cemeteries, singing, praying, and decorating the graves of lost loved ones with these plastic flowers made real by the sentiment they symbolized: their eternal bloom a hope for heaven). The statue before me, in the eyes of someone who grew up around the commitment of his own country's rural city squares to display customary War Memorials, reproducing whatever historical conflict was viewed most significant to the tiny communities they served, was commonplace enough to have hardly rendered an impression, until I stepped closer.

As I peered over another gate, one I dared not circumvent lest I step upon a grave, I was struck, both by the sadness of this soldier's gaze and the deep bow of his downcast, helmetless head. Time and erosion had amplified both.

The degeneration of what was meant to outlive the lives of the bones buried beneath me, coupled perhaps with the added significance of standing, for the first time in my American life, on ground that had itself been fought for during these memorialized battles, made this bare monument provoking past any I'd ever seen. I wondered, as I believe many do when they are new to an old land, why we, humanity, are so keen on attempting eternity, when we know so maddeningly-well the monuments will last no longer than our bones, that, eventually, both the memories of those who were buried here will perish, as will the memorials erected in their memory.

I wrapped my hand around a tree branch and plucked several strong leaves, which I cracked, folded, then dropped in quick and uniform succession, a habit I sometimes catch myself in when lost in thought. Between the first and third handful, I wondered why we insist on fighting a battle we are certain we will never win? Gazing at this decrepit shrine, which welcomed its first visitor in several years, which was punctuated by a church soon to crumble into its own lush burial ground, which was surrounded by names on limestone, carved deeply enough into a material hard enough that these testaments too would last long enough to be forgotten, I couldn't help but wonder why I was there, why any of us struggle to be remembered or sacrifice for a greater cause, when we know one day the cause will cease to be great, and the memory of the last person or the last memorial to remember us will be very distant indeed. Can three generations hold any light to immortality? Am I the intent of these efforts? Was the purpose of all this masonry that a young man from halfway around the world bear witness to their decay, and leave without any better understanding of the individual lives for whom these stones were erected?

I apologize if any of these questions elicit the contained existential crisis it wrought that day on my tired, sweltered mind. As I said before, I struggle to tell you what is happening in my life without letting some of what happening from my life get caught up in the recollection. Though, especially in these first letters, I've made several efforts to exclude what might not be worth saying, the reappearance of these notions seems to denote a subconscious belief that they are as much a part of the story as the place and events which led me to them. I will, therefore, continue to include as much context around the character of these circumstances as my memory of them allows for. If the internal dialogue ever overtakes the narration, however, please remind me of what it is I owe you, and I will do my best to curtail those reflections I remember for my own benefit.

Regaining the moment: I was in an old cemetery, replete with those end-of-life ruminations always conjured by old places or graveyards, and certainly by those graveyards that are themselves old. But the day was beautiful, and near the branch I had just stripped was an inquisitive praying mantis, whose cocked head expressed his confusion at his stripped neighborhood. I chuckled, and apologized for prematurely exposing him to the elements, well before Fall took those leaves for itself.

It was clear this beautiful insect was living for something as it crawled to a new, better-concealed hunting grounds as fast as his prodding pincers would carry him. It was clear the busying babucya (the term lovingly bestowed on any Eastern European grandmother, of such strength of character and archetype they have become their own cultural icon) in the avenue beyond the gate, who caught my attention with a flurry of dusty robes and terse, scurrying strides, was living for something, hurrying along the dirt street with her hands full of reused plastic bottles she'd likely employed in her street-side vender service for as many years as I'd been alive. It was clear, in the background of my insectile contemplation, that the line of barely-perceptible and quintessentially-boxy Lada cars, parked astride one another on the road which I'd left to reach the hill's base, were living for something, waiting for their owners to return them home. Though, as they too had most likely been in use before I'd existed, I was wondered how much longer they would be able to do so.

Home, for these cars, and their passengers, was a jutting column of apartments with facades as sharp and grey as an unimaginative Lego set for the colorblind. These brutalist buildings dotted the landscape and, especially against the lush countryside which appeared by all accounts exactly as quaint and green and rolling and soft as it had for hundreds of years, lent a post-apocalyptic impression to the scene, filling me with an ever-expanding wonder for the strangeness of what my life had become to me. I panned from these beautifully depressive abodes, up from the view of the countryside I had all but ignored since summiting the church's hill, and I saw the sun, and I saw it was clear I was living for something.

Yes, I may be nothing more than a reorganization of molecules that had existed for billions of years and will get along fine without me. Certainly, no matter how many of these letters I write, someone will, eventually, be the last to read them. One day, you and I and whatever we thought we knew will not only be gone, but erased. Yet, the praying mantis lives on, the grandmother lives on, the cars live on, brutalist architecture lives on, the resplendent countryside lives on, the sun lives on, I live on, and the whole mass of this world and its inhabitants, both born and created, plods along its blind course, moved by the unstoppable momentum of life.

Who am I to question that?

When I stumbled into this conclusion, staring at a sun which looked to have transitioned from falling to setting, and decidedly late for my tutoring appointment, the evocative first notes of *Feels Like Summer* (by Childish Gambino, you know, the musician I tried on several occasions to convince you was worth my adoration of his artist) tolled, and their memory made me smile. These tender notes I projected onto my moment harmonized seamlessly with the scene, and with what I imagined having once been the voice of the slender, decaying bell tower behind me, chiming and clanging the tonally-low energy which filled the whole of the valley below. Never had I more poignantly felt the beautiful melancholy of late summer, the comfortable and dreamy sadness of the Earth in its perfectly satisfied atmosphere, where all of its inhabitants lazily sigh under the oppression of a long sun and sink into the comforts of the bountiful season, that polar opposite of a cold dawn, when the world is in sharp relief against itself and yawns hungrily, angered by a clouded sky and the chilly suspension of spring.

The scene was, in a word, replete, and once I'd leapt over the gate, hummed softly while I walked back.

I know you can't hear this music as it sounded in my mind. I know you can't listen to the parsed, awkward conversation I shared with a woman at the bottom of the hill who took my muteness for politeness and, in offering me a piece of candy for even trying to say "hello", singlehandedly renewed the zeal I'd arrived in her country with, an optimism I'd since misplaced within the flurry of culture shock and the stress of the unknown. I know you can't see the scene I paint, no matter how staggering the word count, or how many times I reference Thesaurus.com.

I know I have the benefit of being there, of seeing these things firsthand, of experiencing these second-hand experiences, and recalling the scenes from those neurons reserved for my most profound of memories. You, on the other hand, have the disadvantage of my insufficient writing. I am only able to squeeze from my overly-analytical brain enough of a story because, deep down in places I am too stubborn to see, I know there is no way for me to depict a view like the one I enjoyed that afternoon, to capture the sensation of bounding down a hill in the midst of a perfectly foreign country, to recreate the peculiarity of the person whom I encountered at its base. There is no means by which these moments can become your own. They will always be mine and will be glimpsed through the obscurity of personal understanding by anyone else. In this hopeless context, however, I can ignore my perfectionism, and appreciate the power in my altogether poor attempts at narration.

Because there is, I hope, a power in what I will tell you. There is a power in all stories. We share our experiences, we tell our story, not only to remember it for ourselves, but to aid the listener, the reader, you, in rediscovering their own. In this, each of us reawakens that force which first beckoned us towards individuality, a force which some call wanderlust, some call ambition, and some simply know how to utilize without ever needing a label. This force that was and will always be the impetus behind every attempts, both great and subtle, at what may one day comprise our legacy. When I share with you my collection of moments from Ukraine, I am reminded of why I came here, and, if I relate these with sincerity, will remind you of your own why, of the grandiosity of your own life, and the necessity of seizing what little cosmic coincidence you have to shape reality until we all share the fate of that fallen, forgotten soldier.

So, Michelle, when I write about this picturesque, singular, afternoon, or when I tell you various subplots and little precious instances of my first months here, stories which I could title "My

Fear of Ice Cream Sticks, or watching Ukrainian Dr. Phil and How I Learned to Love Bad TV" and "The Caterpillar and the Babucya", or introduce with purposefully-insufficient summaries like "the time I was confronted with the strangeness of running to run" or "that trip to Kyiv which turned into an adult sleepover and ended with my most harrowing of fecal experiences to date (refer to little updated poop blog)" and, in my opinion, most tantalizingly, "the moment when I got lost on a drunk walk home and was chased by stray dogs and children until hunted down and recalibrated by a worrying host-mom's best friend", I do so, of course, to finally honor the promise I made to you: that I would live these years apart to the fullest, for both our sakes, and that I would keep you a part of my life through a retelling of its highlights. Simultaneously, however, I share these moments to encourage self-reflection in both of us, and even more so, perhaps, in the hopes of bolstering you towards your own colorful collection of escapades and mishaps.

I hope to be reading about them very soon.

Expectantly,

Sam

3.

"Breath in the sweet air of limitless possibility,
and make life as rich as you know it can be."

Ralph Marston

Dear Michelle,

First impressions rarely live up to the ones we imagine, don't they? That's not to say these encounters between expectation and reality are disappointing; if everything was what we expect we'd all be listless savants who never do anything at all. There would be nothing to discover, in each other, in the external.

Do you remember when we met on the rooftop of our college dorm, each of us with the friends we had gone to the freshmen bars with in the hopes of channeling group confidence and the alcohol from the drinks purchased with fake I.D.s into a successful conversation with the opposite sex? The night was warm, late, and our crowds clashed in the common area, the staging grounds for a last, anxious effort to break from our friends. Impelled by the seeming chance of a commonplace encounter, drunk companions seeking companionship, we contrived to make the night memorable, and loudly snuck through the battered, summer-weary garden outside the window to scramble up the façade of our building. Reveling in the thrills of unchecked youth, we ignored the security cameras, glass eyes observing a familiar scene with little interest. Though once and always a naïve romantic, even I could not have thought of a setting more conducive to the aesthetic of a coming-of-age tv drama, a setting more befitting a love's beginning.

We met because we paired off, and we talked because there was little else to do. On a forbidden rooftop, the excitement is in getting there. As the space grew quiet, the other new couples disbanding or coming to immediate fruition somewhere in the building behind us, you and I talked until we were alone.

Our conversation, one I will always remember, had evolved past a point of comfort, I think less out of my willingness to approach authenticity and more because we had finally exhausted anything that saved me from introspection, covering the topics and practiced responses I'd relied on to cement the new impression I'd fashioned for Tallahassee and hoped to impart here. We talked about our real interests, and found they were mutual. I think we kissed, but that's not the part I remember. I remember the way you talked about Whitman, the enthusiasm you had for your major, the way I struggled to give a satisfactory answer to any question of merit, and how I shared little of your optimism for the purpose of our presence in this place. I think back to that night often, and wonder where I'd be if I recognized then the disregard I had for the specifics of my educational autonomy, and whether I'd have chosen differently where I more aware of the apathy I had for formal learning. When we finally clambered back to the ground it was hours yet before I came back to Earth. We exchanged numbers and we said goodbye, and we left for our respective rooms. Yet, I fell asleep sometime later, still quite drunk, and unexpectedly content.

Despite the subsequent color of our context since applied atop the moment, when I learned you spoke, as the campus debriefed the night in the various cafeterias, over afternoon carton eggs and cheap fruit, with your friends about how pretentious I seemed, and that the poem I'd recited from my high school speech class and saved in my notes sounded much better in my own ears, despite the intoxicating embarrassment I felt when this effect found its way back to me, I hold firm to the belief that had we met in any other circumstance, and in any other way, I would not be writing these letters to you. Strangely, the imperfection of my first impression, once which had every chance at being perfectly and forgetfully cinematic had my inner voice proved externally stimulating, had I been a better writer, and started us on this path, the winding relationship which had led us here. I would endure any amount of retrospective cringing for the friendship we've created, and presently enjoy.

In much the same way, Ukraine has proffered a first impression so vastly unlike what I had expected this experience to be, that I know I will cherish the memory of these moments for as long as I live.

For myself, the first months in this foreign place have been riddled with interactions like our first, "delivering an unsolicited and inebriated rendition of Rudyard Kipling's If to a romantic interest whose own interest is diminishing with every syllabic, strident conjunction" kind of moments. Be they the simple, commonplace: the inevitable inelegance of daily life in a place wholly unfamiliar to oneself, times when I brought the wrong currency to the store or, while preparing an early morning omelet, flipped my Russian grandmother's cast iron pan with a vigor it had not seen in years and broke the handle clean off from what would otherwise have been a family heirloom, showering her immaculate stovetop in yolk and green pepper, or the more complex, outside of routine or triviality: the clumsiness of six recent graduates from vastly different walks of life, six personalities in degrees of self-assuredness ranging from jean skirts to a full college freshman-esque chaotic character reset, compelled to spend nearly every waking moment with each other, whose interrelationships were either hampered or intensified in the crucible of an alien environment's perpetual stress, there have been countless awkward moments since we last wrote.

Yet, I am happy in these stories, for from our example, I am assured each of them will survive as a painfully pleasant memory. I see the reflection of our survival in each other's lives in my training cluster, six strangers once and colleagues with varying degrees of annoyance with, contempt for, and reliance on one another first, who have become in the space of a few months some of the closest friends I've ever had. I've told you about my eternal jealous towards those for whom home was a single place, who had the chance at a friend since birth, but here I've made my own. This group I knew from its infancy, these people I've known from their second birth, albeit an effective one, with them I've learned to speak, dress, eat and act in accordance with the culture of our new country. I will cherish them as much as the place which brought us together.

But this episode of my life does not conclude with them.

Continuing on impressions: In essence, my first impression of Ukraine was twofold.

I had the experiences I've related, and met these people I've befriended. Yet, three months after I arrived, during which I discovered some semblance of comfort in the daily language training, cultural classes, cooperative meetings with host country nationals in both the private and public sectors, English clubs, and dinners with Nina, I was once more removed from every notion of familiarity to the degree of separation of a sixteen hour train ride.

In this second first meeting, this second, separate experience, this second Ukraine, here, in a small village on the extreme western border of the country, isolated from the friends I'd made in training and hours away from any other American, comfort and familiarity I found first have proved much more elusive.

I'm sure if I narrated what was a blind date with my Ukrainian counterpart[1] in a train car while a very large, in size and sense, couple watched our terse interactions and finally, either weary of the atmosphere of discomfort or finally succumbing to their copious consumption of water bottle vodka, boisterously challenged the unlike pair before them to a game of cards called Дурак[2][3], no matter how many pages I devoted to the experience, I could never capture the scene satisfactorily. You would be left with

---

[1] Imagine a colleague, translator, and tour guide all wrapped in one literally life-saving business formal dress

[2] "Fool"

[3] Incidentally, I discovered the game to be aptly named, because I have undergone no small distress in my struggle to recall a time when I felt more a fool than during those hours of insistent entreaties to drink alcohol I could barely keep down while consistently losing at a game I barely understood with a companion whom I barely knew, and then only as a coworker)

several burning questions, and, unfortunately, we would be at the mercy of our medium. Were I to try and anticipate those inquiries, the full story would serve only to elicit further demands for explanation, and we would spend the next weeks and no small budget of postage attempting to depict or clarify what was essentially a rift in everything I thought I understood to be time and space. Perhaps, to summarize, a fever dream is a more appropriate analogy than a blind date. Regardless, in an effort to corral my verbosity, your curiosity, and keep these writings in minimal accordance with the current events of my life here, I'll skip the train, the stupor of my first encounter with host national's alcohol tolerance, the initial and frantic days at my site (of which I can concretely recollect very little, my mind far too overwhelmed to form detailed, or even cogent, memories) and my walks about my new home, to impart upon this letter a first impression story, one perhaps more painfully-imperfect than our own, hoping it illustrates the greater point I am trying to make and cuts the word count.

* * *

It was a cloudless day. I remember the light was blinding while I sipped microwaved espresso and tried to bring myself into awareness of the room.

This was the road-facing bedroom of a small house near the top of the village's largest hill. Perechyn rests within the foothills of the vast Carpathian mountain range, and most of its residential buildings, constructed decades before I existed, climbed the gradual slopes of the once-grassy knoll at whose feet the town was formed. Were it not for its unfamiliar architecture, the aggressively bright paper billboards, border police sporting battle tested Kalashnikovs, the unpaved byways, and an extra block of wood nailed askew onto the large cross astride a nearby summit (the orthodox Catholic cross, unlike those in the West, bearing a third beam slanted across the bottom of the upright boards), the locale was reminiscent of many of its Appalachian cousins. The mountains, rounded with age, were canopied by dense forest, and, due perhaps to the visual isolation from the neighboring villages and physical isolation from urban concerns, life moved at a similar, slower pace.

My host parents had roots in these hills deeper than those of the apple tree in their front year, heavy with the unpicked late autumn harvest. The plastic boxes on their stone patio, bearing indecipherable remnants of the local dairy company's logo, were already bursting with an overripe assortment of the fruit we'd eaten as a baked dessert every night since my arrival. In these boxes, coupled with Nina's implementation of old rugs nailed to the thin walls of her city apartment to aid in insulation against cold and noise, the man on the marshrutka[4] who had jimmied a Jenga block in the overhead air shaft to bring some small measure of relief to the stifled student commuters, their elder companions harboring a superstition over cross-breezes and were resolutely shutting any of the cracked windows, I was slowly coming to appreciate the inventiveness of Ukrainian recycling. I better understood my Polish grandmother every day I spent in the company of Ukrainians. They embodied her beloved adage of "waste not, want not", and were extremely adept at repurposing household items to fix things myself and most Americans I'd known would consider broken and replaceable.

The old couple, my new host family with whom I shared three meals and seven words a day, were no exception. They made a pot of espresso every other day, and on the mornings when the coffee was not fresh, they simply reheated what was left of the murky water and enjoyed it all the same. Leftovers were abundant, as were jars of home-pickled vegetables of every variety, dried mushrooms foraged by younger family members, dried plums, with which I was caught red-handed late one night when my Special-K Fruit & Yogurt cravings got the better of me, and an assortment of nuts collected from the town square's wild grove.

Aspects of the city I'd enjoyed the most were amplified here, and life had taken an even simpler turn the other side of a cross-country train ride.

---

[4] Eastern European short bus. Look it up, you will not be disappointed by a cursory Google image search

This morning I sipped stale grounds from a mug that was maybe microwavable safe in the bright sunlight of my eastern window, I watched the neighbor's dog stretch in preparation for its daily pedestrian accosting, and worried over my afternoon presentation.

My first week within the Perechyn City Council had been an exercise in overstimulation, this, even if I'd been able to understand more than one word in ten of the local dialect. With my counterpart in faithful tow, I had been quite literally paraded from office to office, invariably accompanied by a posse of coworkers and their most curious friends and family, and on this never-ending tour was introduced to what felt an impossible, for the town's size, number of local business owners, I sat in on several meetings while the village council and other VIPs discussed how best to utilize me without my involvement, and I shook more burly, swallowing hands and kissed more well-polished cheeks than in the whole of my life preceding.

Following this welcoming pomp and circumstance, the time had come for me to justify the ado and verify it had not been much about nothing. The town's mayor, a dominating man whose influence rendered the six most recent mayoral elections a formality, had tasked me, through a translator, with creating an auto-biographical slideshow for my new colleagues over the weekend. After going back and forth on how much and which of my selves to present, I settled on ten poorly interpreted slides I felt best occupied a middle ground between friendly icebreaker and professional elevator speech. I was a young volunteer working amongst an average age of at least 40, after all, and I had to reach both the austere men who saw me as a mute child and the gushing women who saw me as an adorable one.

Though brimming with confidence the night before, I felt an intense foreboding as I trotted down my hill, past the furious canine, in the wooden-heeled dress shoes designed for fewer stones, potholes, and mud. The eyes of the windows of the homes I passed held, as they had every morning since I'd arrived, the strangely quaffed foreigner in their lingering view. This morning, through struck by the thrill of birdsong unfamiliar, the impact was transient and quickly overshadowed by the anxiety rooted in my lower intestine.

Mercifully, the rest of the morning proceeded as most have, since. I arrived at my office, a square of a room cut into a square of a building with absolutely no distinguishing features. The department I had been assigned to, The Department of Economic Development, Tourism, International Cooperation, and Grant Writing (Yes, it said all of this on the sign outside our door, and yes, just like the Cheesecake Factory, we occupied multiple roles and accomplished them more successfully than any more streamlined organizations) consisted of four middle aged women, three were Ukrainian and single mothers, the other a stern but married Hungarian one, and, as of a week ago, a recent graduate from Florida State University whose only international experience had been a pilgrimage to Rome and whose immature life experience had been poorly supplemented by fraternity gatherings and table waiting. The physical office space was in the room to the immediate left past a white plastic door that looked out of place and a poor protector within the heavy concrete exterior walls the opening had been hewn from. This self-locking entrance was past an alleyway shared by a factory worker's lunch spot, a sports betting internet café, and an espresso and hotdog stand, and opened onto a few rooms with wildly-divergent public purposes and a private toilet. The main city council building, a dour structure even for Soviet-era architecture, was three kilometers up the road.

Inside, our cramped, four desk room which may have comfortably fit two and a coat rack had been rented for departmental use for six years, since the towns bureaucracy at last exceeded the space provided for it.

This morning, after hanging my coat on my chair, I, as I'd hurriedly learned to do, wiped my shoes with a moist towelette, a habit adopted at the behest of the most effective motivator for new behaviors: public shame. Ukrainian tradition held anyone with dirty shoes in contempt, and after a volunteer friend of mine had been roundly corrected on the state of her footwear I vowed to never make the same mistake.

Shoes clean, I sat down at my corner workspace. From my desk I contemplated a view I was fast becoming used to, a small restaurant which served the best potato dumplings in the vicinity, and, further, an abandoned hotel whose courtyard and functionless fences most of the bazaar vendors would use as a shortcut on their walks to work. Its empty window frames, teen-propelled rocks had long since removed any of their glass, left me to wonder what international funding opportunities I would pretend to research for the next four hours, knowing, and not yet accepting, that my job was not to write grants and that it would become to write grants. Instead, I read the news, and did the crossword, ignorant to the state of affairs my already-handicapped productively boded.

My coworkers joined intermittently once 9:30 had passed, most sporting large bundles of officially stamped papers or heavily dressed children on their way to school. I shared a customary greeting, answered a question or two, then spoke with whosever daughter was in tow of their mother for the morning, both of us for different reasons only able to maintain a level of conversation available to an average 10 year old. When they went out, alone, in the office, I set about the task of looking busy until lunch.

At noon, I began preparing for my daily excursion to the bistro on the second floor of a small shopping complex, where a kind old woman and her two daughters offered quick and homemade traditional dishes for little more than a dollar. While the exchange rate had become extremely favorable to Western currencies since the Maidan revolutions in 2014, to encourage assimilation, Peace Corps volunteers are paid in local currency, and so I ate where the crowds were. This felt a prudent practice; since my arrival I have eaten most of my lunches in the corner of this quaint eatery, listening to a pet bird sing along with the Euro pop music video channel, encased in an increasingly-comfortable demographic of my community: schoolchildren and bus drivers, factory workers and their wives, shoe repairmen and bakery women.

I'd latched the buttons of my laptop bag when my counterpart interrupted, asking where I was going. I asked her to repeat the question. Then I told her I was off to eat, and she explained our office had been invited to a birthday party at the main building, and there was no need for me to get my own lunch. Food and drinks would be provided for us there. So I placed my bag back on the desk and, without opening it again, waited for my colleagues to finish their work. We left some fifteen minutes later, making an odd group of village chic ladies and a young man very out of place, lagging slightly behind and bending his head to facilitate or feign some grasp of their bustling conversation.

My coworkers led me into the City Council proper foyer, past a table holding the Tupperware filled with the town's dead batteries, behind the internationally-funded banner advertising an internationally-funded development initiative from a project which concluded three years before my arrival, down the hallway shared by the mayor's office, the budget office, and the IT office, where twenty pristine internationally-funded iPads sat abandoned for the resiliency of a decades-outdated paper government system, and into the small space for community affairs.

Here, the design motif was indistinguishable from our own satellite workspace, save the older walls and the more lived-in appearance of the furniture. If there was a fire code, the maximum occupancy would have been exceeded by the five members of the department who worked daily within its tight walls, but today, twelve additional employees had crammed into every space available. The party was standing room only, and I, the guest of honor, stood helplessly at the center.

After brief introductions to the coworkers I'd yet to meet, we all shared hugs and handshakes, the intent eyes of the room rendering my well-rehearsed greetings shaky and uncertain, then went on with the event.

On the desk I was pressed against was our lunch, items I have since become all too familiar with, as they are all but essential to any Ukrainian celebration, formal meeting, or neighborly visit. There were several trays of what were translated as sandwiches, but from my American eyes, seemed more like large slices of open face Texas toast, topped with a generous slice of butter and thick cuts of market sausage. To their right were a few dozen mandarin oranges, a small plate of shortbread cookies, and, to wash it all down, three tall bottles of local cognac and a 0.5 liter of Coca-Cola, should any of the women choose a chaser.

Proceedings commenced with a short speech from the mayor, who ducked a head into what little space remained to offer a few words and to drink to the health of the birthday girl before heading to other business. He was followed by other short speeches of appreciation and encourage from each of the celebrant's direct coworkers, her department head, her office mates, her childhood classmate, and my counterpart. Each well-wish was toasted. Fifteen minutes into the birthday party, a lunchtime, workplace birthday party, I was six healthy shots of liquor deep. The cognac, potent as any vodka, shared the stomach space with the half sandwich I'd been able to wolf down after toast #3 in a paltry effort to soak up whatever the heavy bread could, and a sip of soda I'd been able to sneak from someone's cup while the room's attention was directed elsewhere. My acclimation, including my taste and tolerance for pure, unadulterated Ukrainian cognac, was, to this point, incomplete, and my taste buds and sobriety were desperate for any measure of relief.

As a graduate of the Florida State University, a former fraternity member, and 150 pounds that you are well aware I had always considered fairly-alcohol friendly, I surveyed the space, expecting my fellow celebrants to be similarly reeling from our mutual and rapid dosage. My assessment left me dumbfounded. From the brief glance, it appeared I was the only one among us whom the shots had affected.

My counterpart, a tall but particularly slender individual, remained as upright and as composed as ever. The men in the room were as stoic as they had been before the drinks, and the women no more expressive in their conversations. The atmosphere was unflinching, calmly celebratory, with no measure of looseness or unprofessionalism. It was all rather business-like, formal, and commonplace. I've since discovered Ukrainians drink with the same determined composure with which they face everything in their lives, and while they all know how to enjoy themselves, alcohol is of no more note at these gatherings than are the oranges, the sandwiches, or the cookies.

Cookies which were, incidentally, the second most popular item on the table and were still only a quarter eaten by the time two of the three bottles had been emptied and placed back into their owner's reusable shopping bags.

I, to a starkly opposite extent from my coworkers, was panicking.

Though I did my best to denote an equivalent composure, I had become drunk, and was spacing between considerations enough to no longer care what anyone thought of my clutching a cup of soda fuller than when I had poured it. Though my male peers found no small amount of humor or personal satisfaction at my doing so, I was unphased, simply grateful they hadn't been watching me after the last two toasts. Shots #7 and #8 floated on the surface, disguised in the dark liquid. After, through an impaired self-awareness, I felt the level of my beverage had begun to reach a suspicious height in the clear cup, and shot #9 went into the soil of the office plant behind me.[5] Though, by my alma mater, well trained in the art of feigning participation in a drink, shot #10 proved impossible to counterfeit, and I nearly glared at the woman who had kept her gaze on me while it went down reluctantly, with a pained grimace I did my best to hide, but her smile told me she'd spotted.

This last taste of sharp ether pushed me over the proverbial edge, and the party's noise collected itself into an undistinguishable murmur. Only what I directly focused my attention on existed to me at the time. Remember when I told you that when I drink, I start to feel like I've receded well into the back of my own head, viewing my life from a distance, like the emotions in Inside Out? Well, my view was now so removed it had started becoming blurry, and the initial nausea that accompanied any straight alcohol I'd ever consumed had ceased to fade away and remained resolute against the sandwiches I sent in after it. It was clear I had to escape,

---

[5] Upon the first effects of the alcohol, I had retreated to a more advantageous position in the room, away from the center and against a bookcase to the left of the activity. The last thing I wanted was to be discovered wasting cognac

so, as incognito as my position allowed, I snuck out to find the restroom.

The building was mercifully empty, and I was allowed to stumble to the second floor anonymously.

The men's bathroom of Perechyn's City Council was something out of a movie, one not very pleasant for its protagonist. Think the Saw franchise, an ideal scouting location for an Eastern European installment. Two out-of-use urinals were bolted to the wall, a third, without a garbage bag draped over it, softly gurgled with the steady stream of a leaky pipe. A single stall stood precariously adjacent to the mirror and sink immediately to my right. The grime on the glass, the rust on the faucet whose handles were missing, and the state of the porcelain were all accentuated by the dripping water splashing on a dirty drain. A few weeks from this moment I will learn that this particular restroom is, by all accounts, condemned. A much more comfortable facilities option beckons, mere steps down the hall.

This afternoon, however, the day's bright summer sun and the fresh countryside breeze through the open window were this dungeon's saving grace, a glaring contrast to its grimy impression, and I quickly ran to thrust my head through the frame to drink the blessed relief of crisp air, the kind that fills you from the top of your skull and sweeps down your spine on its way into the lungs, bringing rejuvenation wherever it went. The breeze was as near Ralph Marston's "sweet air" as I'd ever experienced. I drank my fill gratefully, and once the breath's restorative effects returned me to my present, I felt sober enough to take in the rest of my surroundings.

I was both unsurprised and horrified to see a very old woman staring directly up at me from a distance of about three feet. The fence of her backyard was the rear wall of the government building. I could hear her neck creak as she paused her chicken feeding to regard the stranger sucking air above her. We shared a lingering moment of flabbergasted eye contact, then I ducked inside, and she returned to her coop.

When I returned to the party, there were several inquiries I had to dodge before I learned the lunch period was nearly over, and my presentation would begin shortly thereafter. I asked my counterpart what room I should look for to set up, and she laughed. The town's projector was in the hotel across the street, and how else would I give a presentation? I gulped, took as generous a drink of the bracingly warm mineral water as my evolutionary human fear of drinking salt water would allow, and followed my cohort out of the building.

Hotel Beriska was as predictably eclectic as this story may have led you to believe. Its outer walls were lime green and topped by a white border in the image of a castle rampart, its foyer replete with faux wood and dark furniture of the kind uniquely at home in places that rarely saw visitors, the staff desk was vacant, and the conference hall through the double doors was little more than what you may expect a basement cafeteria of a small middle school to resemble. The chairs were set up in neat rows, however, and astride the projector was a small table of sandwiches and cookies, which terrified me. Hor'doeuvres meant an event, and if this was to be an event, there was more than a slight possibility I had misunderstood my purpose within it.

Nevertheless, I promptly realized I could do nothing to rectify my misjudgment, and even if I had the time, I was honestly too intoxicated to care.

Whatever happened was going to happen.

Once we finally figured out the cables, our guests started to arrive, and soon all 30 of the chairs were taken, and a small group of people I had never seen stood in the rear of the room without a place to sit. The volume of their expectant conversation washed over me with the force of something it was too late to avoid, and I eagerly sought my counterpart's reassuring look, who had vanished amongst the crowd.

Here I was, swaying before the next two years of my life, overdressed and underprepared, very buzzed, the whole array of kind gazes and the less-enthused mayoral cabinet waiting, slowly coming to silence. My time had come. I welcomed them all in their native tongue and introduced myself exactly as I had already done on dozens of occasions, no deviation from the essential script, as if I were a captured soldier robotically repeating his name, nationality, and purpose to the microphone and one-way mirror. With my prepared remarks exhausted, banal words about my first week in their town which elicited a comforting level of chuckling, I braced myself. My life, my Peace Corps service, my work in this town, hung in the balance. Once I pressed the tiny black remote in the sweaty palm of my right hand, there would be no going back. The first formal impressions would be made, the group judgement rendered. The mayor of our little world sat up straighter, prepared to dictate the reactions of his government.

I pressed the right arrow, setting in motion several things, which all happened in an instant.

First, an adorable photo of me as a toddler sprang onto the screen. Second, I recognized, by the mayor's near-immediate facial response, the inclusion of this picture had been a mistake. Third, a few of the older women proffered a sympathetic "awh". Fourth, the whole of the group were largely unimpressed, as directed by their boss. Fifth, I remembered that I had plugged my entire presentation through Google Translate, and had next to no idea what the slide said. Sixth, I began speaking, in English, without a soul in the room willing or qualified to translate.

Had I been sober, this damning combination of missteps would surely have driven me from the stage. But the cognac was within me, and, oblivious to my audience, who understood nothing, save the rather untimely picture of some baby playing with a hose they had to assume was me, I spoke about my hometown, my childhood, my family, the origins of the individual who wanted to travel the world and who volunteered to come and share his life with them. Eventually, likely due to overwhelming discomfort, my counterpart began translating, but by that time, I had already lost them.

As I switched to the second slide, displaying a picture of my family, the Denver skyline, and some words about life in America, the mayor, followed shortly by his advisory staff, pushed their chairs away and made a raucous show of leaving the hotel. I saw them in the bay window by the hospitality station, and was unable to speak until they'd disappeared from sight.

Again, had I been lucid, I may have been able to understand the significance of this moment. I had yet to grasp the lingering cultural effects of a Soviet government structure, though, and this is a discussion better suited for a phone call. In the moment, I simply offered an ignored goodbye and thanks for attending, then proceeded with the auto-biography. By the time I reached the slide detailing my career achievements, my professional skills, and my ideas on how to best utilize the two years, the expected purpose of this meeting, my audience was halved.

When it was over, I received some congratulations from my officemates, but it was clear these were ceremonial. Their supervisor's exit was not lost on them. The context, their expressions, and the emptiness of the room were well and thoroughly missed by a young man who happily received their compliments, focused entirely on the relief from the conclusion of his first international presentation.

*   *   *

If you read this as my friend it may be tempting to feel bad for me. Upon rereading, even I feel bad for the luckless, ignorant idiot I've created on these pages. Please do not, Michelle.

Though I, of course, have spent considerable time considering how I might change certain aspects of the experience, if I could, I don't think I would. Though there are a million other ways I would rather have introduced myself to my new world, I am grateful for the story, and optimistic the introduction will not overshadow my cooperation.

I arrived in Ukraine with a head of lofty expectations, filled with myriad fantasies. Had these been enough, I never would have come. An imagined perfect life is enough to keep us from living the imperfect real one.

I'm sure you remember my vastly unsettled notions of what this would all be like, and wonderfully, I was completely wrong about them all.

If the ideas we hold of our future remain intact, then we did not live them.

I celebrate these awkward moments and these awful first impressions exactly because I could never have anticipated them. Slowly, with every passing day, I am losing the ideas of this experience and gaining the reality of it. I am much, much better for this. I hope this story is proof as much. I hope it evokes laughter, appreciation for life's ambiguity, and a wry smile, your yourself all too aware of my inexplicable penchant for finding myself in moments like these. I hope sympathy never enters your consideration.

Lastly, truly, while I am certain the theme of this story will not be the norm, I am reminded of how dangerously easy it is to lose track of time when you have better days ahead. I hold these moments in my mind, reflect on them through my keyboard, and catch myself looking forward to the day when I am comfortable in this village. I know this is a mistake. Often in my life I have fallen prey to this longing, the idea that things will be better in the future, and with my mind in the unknown I missed a lot of what was happening around me. Once my future is tangible enough to welcome foresight, I am absorbed by an active imagination.

It overtakes, often swallows, my present.

Even here, at times throughout my nascent Peace Corps service, I have sensed this. How could I stay focused on my language classes when finally about to transition to the life I'd signed up for all those months ago? How could I invest in relationships I was certain to lose when our training ended? However, here, it seems the intensity of this irreplaceable experience has at last woken me up to the futility of looking forward. I understood, in this depth of every moment, that those people in my training group, those Americans who became some of my closest allies, were whom I had come for as much as any of the service to Ukraine, as essential to this life as the host country friends and colleagues I'd expected to befriend and work with. The daily shock of my unfamiliar environment showed me I was soon to fail once again to invest in friendships as I ought, and, had my time with them not been so defined, I might have missed the rewards and joys of three months of my life simply because I was meant to be preparing for the following twenty-four. I hope, holding this, that the life-changing nature of my time abroad, as it was advertised to me by everyone I met who had ever done something like this, might prove so, and will include a lasting change to the commitment I make to my present.

I facilitate this transformation with each letter I write to you. The words tie me to the current, and your name at the top of the page reminds me of the necessity of this personal growth. I choose to write to you because I want to. I choose to stay alive to you because I wish to. Please continue to write back, and, in doing so, hold me accountable to what I have set out to accomplish, both here, and there.

I look forward the impressions mine have upon your own.

Presently,

Sam

4.

"Once you get through that terrifying threshold of accepting that, every place is the center of the universe, every moment is the most important moment, and everything is the meaning of life"

Dan Harmon

Dear Michelle,

In my last letter, I opined on how I'm slowly losing the idea and gaining the reality of this experience. In this one, I hope you'll let me expound.

I'm not sure if you remember, sitting with me on that stiff couch, the last of my furniture to leave the apartment, small and stark-white without the fixtures of home, my vastly different notions as to what this would all be in practicality. Over jasmine tea and a show neither of us were watching I suggested a thousand ways in which the Peace Corps would reward me, a thousand circuitous justifications, a thousand evasive excuses for my leaving.

As I mentioned, I have been wonderfully wrong at every turn. While the imperfections of real life can, by life's very nature, never live up to the movie-like, perfect-to-the-point-of-oblivious expectations in my head, I am much, much better for having lived through the raw footage.

Stories are mined from experiences, when, in hindsight, the plot points are clear and the ending they lead to, definite. Though one day my mind will edit these moments, context and nostalgia will gloss over their worries, and in memory they will recapture the limiting purity of my foresight, as sad as losing so much of the moments for the sake of their story will be, I thought that, through this letter, I might immortalize some measure of those details that will be abandoned for a more coherent picture. I thought that, with these pages, I could flesh out my present, present a few gritty details and some less eventful triumphs, and give you a more complete picture of life here through its small moments. I thought I could share a few shorter recollections, for you and for their perpetuity, and in these, endeavor to reassure you my departure from our life was not merely to be drunk at noon and stumble through biographical presentations, or to suffer through fresh crises of identity with every clumsy conversation.

I came here to live, and life is far more beautiful, far more tangible, in the anecdotes I would never think to send the thousand miles between us.

I've compiled a few of them below.

* * *

"When you rely on something different to be something special, you are sure to miss the beauty of everyday life"
— *Me, sometime in college when I was high and furiously creating platitudes in my phone notes*

I am living on my own now, in a small apartment to the west of the village center.

The complex I call home is everything horribly wonderful about Soviet architecture, an enticing in its dour effect drab gray block of uniform windows and double faux-wooden doors. Surrounding the building is a dirt road shared by myself, several stray dogs, clusters of local chickens, and the other commuters, those who also work in the town proper or the factory on the outskirts. All of us do our best to avoid the resilient puddles of rain water which last until the next mountainous downpour. In the courtyard, in front of a few unmarked parking spaces, is the quintessential communist playground, complete with a rusted merry-go-round, spray painted tires, and a hand-welded swing set. The few boxy vehicles alongside belong to the families upstairs, whom I see rarely. In all, I've met members of four different households. I am as yet unaware if we share the apartments with anyone else, but the quiet and the sparse signs of life outside makes me believe there are many unoccupied rooms.

Behind the building is a stunning Ukrainian Orthodox church built in the traditional Carpathian style, whose gilded roof and log siding shines in stark contrast to the deteriorating neighborhood in which it was once centered. The grounds behind its high fencing are the only in the area that display any amount of lawncare, likely as the unique place of worship serves as most frequented of the town's three landmarks, the others being the country's second-largest horseshoe monument and a statue of a famous postman who, as legends have it, gave his life on a cold winter's morn to the once noble profession, and so the church must exhibit the combined care and attention given to either god or tourists.

From my front door, I climb down stone stairs whose walls are painted green to chest height, and are white and chalky above, and exit through a pitch black foyer where my mailbox waits, unused. I retrieve your letters directly from the post office. Outside, the few meters of sidewalk take me around to the front, where the concrete ends at the main path into my small subdivision, which intersects with the village's main and single throughway street. I walk past my first-floor patio, accessible to anyone of average height or a modest jump, which I have lined with broken glass per my counterpart's recommendation. Thirty minutes ago, from this vantage point a person might enjoy an uncomfortably-close eye contact with a strange, foreign-looking man in a bathrobe sipping his morning coffee in the apartment that was, until a few weeks ago, always vacant, for security reasons. I step underneath my balcony and turn towards the train tracks, careful to avoid the eggshells I've dropped and the bowl of milk I keep filled for the stray cats.

The old woman across the hall usually leaves some sausage for the dogs, and between us and whoever is putting out the fruit and vegetable compost, we keep our building's communal pets well fed.

A block of little storage sheds lays directly to my left, their sheet metal construction leaving several gaps through which the alley-cats relentlessly pursue Carpathian fowl. These dominate the view from my balcony, and are all I can see when visibility is poor, and the mountains are hidden in the low clouds. Inside of one of the metal cubes is the apartment dumpster, which I have vowed to visit and can only brave once the sun has set and the refuse oven has had time to cool. Amidst their rusty roofs protrudes a hollowed out grain elevator, a tall brick tower long without a purpose and popular with the neighborhood's teens. Gopniks, I believe they're called, the ones who wear track suits exclusively and have perfected the Slavic squat at an early age. I was initially disappointed when I snuck inside this tow one evening and found the stairs had been destroyed or crumbled in several places, and without a Bruce Wayne-like effort and an imprisoned crowd chanting me on there was no way I was going to reach the top. On further inspection, I noticed this obstacle existed in the best interest of both health and safety, as the structure's slow tilt was much more apparent inside, and the stench of cigarette ash, hormones and a shockingly well-preserved pile of human feces ensured this was a place I needed only to see for myself once. On future investigations into the abandoned places of Ukraine, I made sure to keep my eyes on the ground in front of me.

Once I've left my building it's a 20 minute walk to work, but the landscape changes quite dramatically in those few kilometers (or fewer miles if my use of the metric system is too pretentious).

Aside my route, were this a late morning and the weather temperate, I might spot the man who runs an appliance resale business from his garage setting out his modest collection of used bicycles. I've been tempted to buy one, but can never remember the word for bicycle when I see him, and, instead, I usually offer a friendly nod and a smile while he asks if I'm interested, and how the microwave I bought from him is working. I have memorized how to say "my food is very hot" at least. I don't know if he finds humor in the phrase or in the observation that I don't know anything else to say. I've made peace with either, as long as he isn't laughing at my pronunciation.

Further along the path are other residential homesteads, houses boasting beautiful second-floor balconies and wrapped by the gorgeous wrought-iron gates I mentioned before and seem a staple of domestic Ukrainian life. Most of the yards double as farmland, and no matter the time of day, I will invariably meet the eyes of the tired old dog who belongs to the house second from the intersection on the right, who either smells and awaits my arrival or is forever in his familiar place atop the mossy roof of his kennel. His tired old owner also rarely moves, and I can rely on her reading a newspaper on the sunlit patio. Both are creatures of fierce habit, but she usually has more important things to look at, and has never met my silent greeting.

Adjacent her house is a family-owned shop, a re-purposed mother-in-law suite offering essential goods to the homes in the radius between it and the identical businesses both a few minutes' walk up and down the street, complete with several sponsored fridges, a home deep freezer, makeshift countertop, eclectic bags and boxes and crates of goods deemed saleable by the shopping habits of neighbors, and the best selection of cherries in season. Beyond its sphere of dedicated customers are other stores which serve other functions, and though each of these makeshift markets are owned and operated by the families who live in the households behind them, they face little competition from each other. The model would never work in the States, but here patrons are fiercely loyal and ignore price for convenience and, even more so, for camaraderie. My counterpart, whose father is a kind of local tycoon and owns three of these stores, taught me the key to navigating this plethora of mom and pop groceries is to learn what each is famous for by watching where and what the old women buy and compartmentalizing your shopping list accordingly.

This becomes especially important in that what you can find in these stores is generally consistent. Fresh produce is available in the form of stalwart staples whose plants are in season year round, ingredients essential to Ukrainian cuisine such as potatoes, carrots, onions, and cabbage. Alongside are 10 pound bags of other veggies, frozen and mixed, various shapes of pasta, a generous selection of Roshen candies and chocolates, milk packets, sour cream packets, butter packets, and kefir packets, basically any liquid or semi-solid dairy sold in a bag and, of course, every imaginable iteration of bread, baked locally. I imagine this aesthetic of home goods stores with specific offerings sprinkled among the village neighborhoods to be similar to the function of the New York bodegas, though I've yet to visit your city.

In either case, the most remarkable feature of these, or any, local store, is the coffee machine. The Jacobs espresso machine, to be exact. The Ukrainian Nespresso. No matter the product sold, or service offered, be it laundry detergent or shoe repair, there is, inevitably, a 5 hryvnia (about $0.75) espresso available for purchase. These coarse and piquant roasts, hot and ready in a minute, must pair nicely with a thin cigarette, as I've rarely witnessed the two partaken exclusively. Though I assumed a coffee culture so pervasive to be uniquely South American, I have fully embraced Eastern Europe's own chase of the rapid, all-hours buzz.

Inside this particular corner store, I've learned, is the town's best collection of butter and low-fat packets of milk. I've remained reluctant to return, however, as my first attempt left me scrambling for the Google translate app and departing with a kilo of strawberries because I had been too embarrassed to try and correct my original request of a few hundred grams. The visit had consumed nearly a quarter of my monthly budget, and the intensely communal aspect of these places ensured I'd be forever referred to as the "strawberry boy" in the neighborhood. Now, I always walk the extra ten minutes for the central, chain store, which has its own digital register that displays the totals and requires no dialogue. I actually think this cashier, lacking all the domestic charm, prefers I leave my headphones in.

The store where I earned my nickname shares a fence with the village sauna, an establishment frequented year-round by residents of all shapes and sizes and sexes, yet, in the evenings, exclusively by large, boisterous men. I was told I'd soon be attending a birthday party here and I've studied the place closely since, my apprehension for what the event may entail corresponding to the collection of empty vodka bottles accumulated daily in its several wastebins.

When I reach the main road, the single throughway which connects the cities Uzhhorod and L'viv and is flanked by the ancient railway which ferries the 6 AM, noon express, and 8 PM trains, the storied splendor of my Carpathian village is made most apparent. From my curbside contemplation, when the large log carriers, Slovakian semi-trucks, marshrutkas, or Mercedes work vans retrofitted as mercantile transports by artisan import companies do not impede my vision, a stunning panorama of the nearby hills is spread beyond the tracks.

These woods, like much in this ancient land, are old, and possess within them the mystical aura of time and circumstance. Antiquity is abundant in their mountains, centuries-old monasteries raise their bright blue domes through the fog, the resolute walls of a lost Hungarian castle adorn the adjacent peak. Its interior, once a court to princes and nobles, is a favorite for picnics and bonfires. I enjoy reading on the crumbling ramparts when they are silent in the mid-afternoon stillness, the sun baking the stone laid by hands centuries-old. The air in the valley is a fresh hitherto unknown to me, aerated history, scented by wide expanses of aged canopy and underdeveloped settlements. Before work, I will often pause and take in the scene, drinking the pleasant scent of the early breeze. When the sidewalk is empty and the cars sparse, of course. I am still too self-conscious to be an alien witnessed appreciating a scene by anyone who has long since been accustomed to the same.

I turn towards the village and walk astride an abandoned Methodist church, the ill-conceived initiative of an overfunded overseas parish, a hollow structure unable to flourish in exclusively Catholic soil, Orthodox or Roman.

Past this overgrown and once-hallowed ground is one of the last monuments in Ukraine to bear the red star and hammer and sickle of Soviet Russia. A landmark, and a painful memory. On my second day in the village I attended a historical tour of the town, conducted by a professor from the local city of Uzhhorod in dialectic Ukrainian. As a result, I retained little of the descriptions, but the number of stops we made, the number of places with a past, even for this nondescript village of little more than 8,000 people, was enlightening. Here, from what my counterpart was able to translate, I'm fairly certain, is the memorial dedicated to over 200 Soviet soldiers who perished in a train car accident, apparently the single worst train tragedy to befall any European participant in World War 2. The disaster seemed a strange claim to fame, but the monument was erected at the height of the post-war fervor, and still bears the symbols of Ukraine's former and torturous occupier because this village was so far off the map to be of any import to the commission tasked with red star removal.

Though Western Ukraine is certainly the region of the country least sympathetic to their eastern neighbor's influence, despite nearly every resident of this country speaks fluent Russian as either a first or a close second language, and though L'viv is well-known as the Ukrainian city where anyone overheard using Russian runs the risk of being scolded, scorned, or, in some cases, assaulted, Perechynians pride themselves on the unique nature of this memorial, and preserve its significance in a unoffending affront to their region's social-political norms. Anti-Russian sentiment is in the water here, courses through the blood of those who lost grandfathers in the great war, fathers in the Chernobyl disaster, sons in the ongoing war in the occupied territories of Eastern Ukraine[6], yet this single red star remains. Sometimes I'm reminded of the Confederate flags which taint so many of the small, overlooked places of our own homeland as I walk past the stones and graves, on my commute. How many of those Stars and Bars still wave in an effort to preserve ideology or history? How many wave merely because they have done so for so many years? If I polled my community, assuming I had the vocabulary, I imagine most, if not all, would admit an indifference to the small plaque on the edge of town, but if I reported it to one of the nearby city's news stations there would likely be a petition to remove the hammer and the sickle, to paint the star gold, and this would be

---

[6] Incidentally, Ukraine is the only Peace Corps country hosting volunteers while simultaneously being actively engaged in war. During our orientation, we were shown a map of the country, upon which a bold red line had been drawn on the border of the three easternmost oblasts, to accompany an explanation that any crossing into the red zone would constitute an immediate and unappealable removal from the program. Several of my friends from raining lived in what was considered the "yellow zones", but we were not allowed to visit them unless they came West.

accomplished in days. Life moves at a different pace when removed from the sweeping current of the greater world's progress, and what washes up on forgotten shores such as these comprises the mystical nature of these places, and the irony of modern life in an antiquated setting.

Within this realm of incidental preservation are the post-apocalyptic eternal carnivals, prerequisite to many post-Soviet towns, one of which is on my right further up the road. Once an odd fairground-like area, permanent Ferris wheels, merry-go-rounds, and other self-operating mechanical rides for local children, these have since taken on a deeply haunting aura. The rusted gears are conspicuously restless whenever I am near, squeaking memories at me from underneath headless plastic horses. Though my route takes me past a mass tomb of nameless soldiers, past an abandoned place of worship, past a shop where I am forever the butt of a fruitful joke, I quicken my pace only immediate this graveyard of entertainment. There is something so potent in its dichotomy of purpose and effect. It is as if a cemetery is less off-putting because its purpose is to remind us of our mortality, it exists to unsettle. While an abandoned playground's implications to the observer are equally morbid, its delivery is far more subtle, more sinister, and more disturbing. What is left of the bright paint, chipped and falling to a ground where visions of laughing children chase one another, sends a shiver more repellant than any I've feel for death when I was encouraged to. Empty army barracks and the makings of what was once another city center surround the field, but I've already, in my few months, been exposed to sufficient Ukrainian superstitions, some of which have successfully seeped into my perception that they keep me from exploring here.

I keep a wide berth.

Nearer downtown, indications of modern life become more consolidated. Across the village's gas station is a train crossing and a guard station, where border patrol officers lay in wait of any large van riding heavily enough on its axels to warrant inspection. Since Ukraine is not within the EU, and its currency's exchange rate is so favorable, the illegal smuggling (I'm not sure if this is redundant) of goods bought at Ukrainian prices with European cash into Slovakia or Hungary is as rampant through these mountains, as is the corruption which extorts these opportunists. Authorities welcome every chance to elicit bribes from the vehicles that stop when they are flagged down, in official or unofficial capacity. To encourage the drivers to brake when beckoned to, and submit to a search once at a halt, each of these guards sports a fully-operational Kalashnikov, a fact I was made painfully aware of when, in my first week in this new apartment, I was taken for an illegal immigrant and stopped in suspicion. The brutal reality of these weapons I'd only seen in video games made the search for my visa a truly terrifying morning, and the tension galvanized their owners' suspicion. Fortunately, my host mother found out about the incident before I was arrested and before I myself even understood what had happened, because a friend of hers was driving into town behind me. Words carries fast in the village, and faster still when "our American" is involved.

Just beyond the petrol station is Perechyn's leading case for continued existence, a massive eye-sore of a gurgling metal factory which produces, exclusively, to my knowledge, rubbing alcohol. Immense, imposing walls surround the complex, and the only entrance I have found well protected and is the main conduit for the train cars, trucks, and sooty workers who are endlessly pouring in and out. Thus, unlike most of the cavernous structures and derelict manufacturing warehouses, the ghost town of industry which is the deserted half of the village, a dusty, vandalized testimony to the greater community that has long outlived its heyday, I have not explored this structure. Furthermore, the factory, which crashes and clanks and spouts unceasingly, louder in the late hours of the night, oozes a smell so toxic I am forced to seek it a second time whenever I encounter it, one of those sensational mistakes so horrible they must be repeated to ensure their reality, like touching a hot pan twice or compulsively blasting a terrible song on repeat. This stench is so potent, Michelle, that the neighboring towns all refer to Perechyn as "the smelly place", and, when speaking with other Ukrainians about where I live, this is often the first thing they will ask about. I promise this is not the impression of a self-indulgent foreigner. For us, though, we were to turn our noses up at the odor, we'd only smell the more effectively. So, we accept the aroma, and we pray for nose-blindness. I am eager for this relief, but I worry that the more time I spend here, the more I've found myself relying on this punch of pungency to wake me up to the day, and I struggle with the greater evil, that one day I join my fellow villagers for whom it makes no difference, or that one day I leave, and am forced to set off morning fireworks for their sulfur.

Once I cross the unnatural stream of redolent run off, a concrete waterway which dumps directly into the river and is why my mayor is so exceptionally enthusiastic for my work with local youth so that he can have me create photo-ops in the form of an environmental awareness club, and let go of a long-held breath, I am a few precious steps from the office.

Here is often where I will check the time, realize my walk to work has been more a contemplative stroll, and increase my gait, lest one of my coworkers has chosen this characterless morning to be punctual. A small booth of fresh baked pastries relieves my overstimulated nostrils. I've begun to buy my bread here because the woman behind the counter has never commented on my accent. Behind her shop is the restaurant that was the scene of my self-induced man vs food challenge (I know I told you I'd leave out the stories, but, briefly: A few weeks ago, I wandered inside at the behest of a large overhead sign advertising good pizza, and found a modest establishment packed by what must have been half of Perechyn's population. The kind hostess could only seat a single diner at a table that had been reserved for 30 minutes later, and I, of course, having understood none of what she said, realized only once I'd received my large supreme pie that I had five minutes to finish it before I would be removed from the table. I'm sure they used a gentler word than removed, but the translation communicated a proper urgency, and I devoured my order in four and a half minutes, to the shock of the family to my left and the amusement of the students to my right).

Finally, I am there, at the small corner of a small building in a small town in which I live and work. Whenever I arrive, be it 10 minutes early or an hour late, the sprawling maze of Perechyn's bazaar across the street from my office is open and bustling, and tantalizing but for the requisite language level of bartering. Yesterday the blueberries looked especially plump, and I spent most of my morning familiarizing myself with produce weights. The bus station, whose loudspeaker I like to listen to from my desk to practice Ukrainian time-telling, roars a final warning for the 9 o'clock to Uzhhorod. The storefronts, boasting regional fashion options and second-hand household wares, are welcoming and frequented, and the set of pots and matching tea kettle which I have had my eye on for weeks catches my eye, still awaiting my monthly stipend deposit. Everywhere, the streets are replete with the signs of another day in the life of this village, and I head inside.

With a thought for the everyday,

Sam

5.

Dear Michelle,

If I told you I was lonely, would you believe me?

The word itself is strange, the sensation stranger.

With all I have ever thought myself to be, loneliness seemed an emotion I could only experience if it were self-inflicted. An experience to be attained, not recognized. And then, still, not in its entirety. Certainly, the person I purport, the tropes I embody or aspire to, be them "the perpetual new kid in school" or "someone who has never met a stranger", designations given me by circumstance, or "the social butterfly" and "the perfect score on any extroverted personality quiz", individualities I've adopted as a means of self-characterization, would ensure isolation be forever beyond any personal comprehension.

Then I came here.

In the drastic separation from all I'd known, from everything comfortable, and still, then, only once I'd exhausted every online stimulant the overtaxed village Wi-Fi could load and grown accustomed to circumstance and the overwhelming stimuli which bogarted my attention in those early months, did there remain nothing else but to feel the solitude.

Of course, separateness is not to be perfectly equated to loneliness, and there is virtue between the two, but, absent a practiced familiarity with internal discovery, in a broken relationship with silence such that precludes peace in isolation, the two coincide.

For myself, I've found it distressing. You may already be aware, knowing me as you do, of how long I've avoided solitude, and, coincidingly, the work of knowing me. Thinking back on our conversations, I've begun to understand why you were so intent on asking me the questions you did. They were never for you. These inquiries were meant to guide me to a place you knew I was avoiding: a sense of self-awareness I'd convinced myself I could do without. I was happy with who I was, so long as I didn't reflect too much on who that was. The risk of upsetting this internal complacency far outweighed any mental boon I might uncover within the recesses of my consciousness.

I'm sorry it took me so long for me to understand the purpose behind your prodding intent, to recognize the growth you were pleading me towards.

As with so many of these communications, please consider this letter an invitation to a thoroughly-deserved, vindicating, and, I hope, at least partially-comforting last laugh.

I mistook your meaning, and felt the answers demanded by what you asked of me too revealing, and selfishly motivated.

Then, I lived in a small apartment on the outskirts of a Ukrainian village, where nature was my neighbor and language muzzled what I'd always used to escape its quiet.

With little else to occupy my time, bored by over-indulgence in novels and movies and avoidant of social interaction, I'd sit on that small balcony just to be outside. There, though thoughts arose, they were soon depleted. When every imagined distraction was spent, I suppose these moments became a sort of callow mediation. It seemed pervasive boredom had brought me to a place many are capable of finding, much more practically, in a few deep breaths. On these afternoons, the shallow sun reflecting green and blue from the shards of glass atop the railing, I meditated, and I remembered something, perhaps for the first time.

I remembered my personality had been given to me.

Despite a determination for the contrary, I've never looked into a mirror and recognized a person who has never met a stranger. I've never said aloud the words I'd so often relied on to describe myself, nor have I ever appreciated the objective meaning behind them. The very concept of first meeting someone who is not a stranger is a paradox. I've met, and will continue to meet, strangers. This phrase, and the others I've relied on to individualize, were internally applied but externally learned; I did not speak them into my mind nor did I live them into existence. I did not unearth these qualities in myself. Rather, to skirt the arduous process of self-development, I adopted expectations. I adapted to pre-conceived impressions, and I assumed what others saw in me.[7]

If I were looking inward honestly, absent outside influence, an endeavor I'm only now making fledging, accidental afternoon attempts at, I would envision myself a social chameleon, not a butterfly. I do not flit from flower to flower, drawing sustenance from each splendid blossom of unique human connection on which I alight. I move subtly, changing my outward expression to suit a changed environment. Both the butterfly and chameleon are colorful, resilient, and adaptive, but where the butterfly exudes its distinctiveness in every flap of its painted wings, itself resplendent, the chameleon disguises, is in a place as a place and never makes it its own.

There is a reason I prefer to ask questions when meeting new people, rather than answer them. The more I know, the better I can adjust. The more they know, the harder it is to do so.

Then I lived in a place where I could not ask those questions.

How can I assimilate a personality when I can hardly maintain a surface-level interaction, much less an insightful, revealing conversation? Yet, here is where I find myself, a handicapped social chameleon, left wondering who he is when the background fades.

---

[7] As a note, I think it was my mom who gave me this specific iteration, which explains why it rings so boastful upon reflective repetition. A mother's love should always be tempered when personally applied. I shudder to consider the colossal ego I'd be encumbered with if I saw myself exactly how she sees me.

Lost, when there is nothing to be camouflaged to.

The effects of this circumstance are worsened by my pseudo-celebrity status, in the same way that loneliness felt underneath bright windows and amongst a bustling urban sidewalk is more poignant than when it is felt in the depths of a quiet forest, or atop a lonely mountain. In the sun and the city, the irony of isolation is palpable, and heavy, and worsens its consequence. Do you remember in my last letter, when I told you the whole town knew of my run in with the border police before the adrenaline from the interaction had even begun to subside? With my heart pounding, I understood that my every action was made significant in my context.

It's impossible to hide under a microscope, and therein lays my current state of mind.

I don't anticipate having explained my perspective well enough that you might grasp this mentality for yourself, but, optimistic of our past, I will hazard the following hypothetical, regardless: For someone who is a stranger, who has relied almost entirely upon knowing others to know himself and someone who has relied almost entirely upon discovering who others are to form relationships with them, how would this person be sure of himself or connect himself to the world around him when it becomes impossible to elicit any of this knowledge?

For my fellow volunteers who possess a greater self-assuredness, they have found a warm and welcome reception from their communities. They, with little hesitation, have laid bare who they are and shared themselves with a people eager to learn.

My own experience, my assuredness at fault, has been markedly different. What relationships I do claim, have formed from either convenience or necessity. In them, neither party can see in the other more than they must.

While I regularly hear stories of success from volunteers who are themselves, I am still working on self-discovery, and often, on slow days in the office, I buy myself time by listening to podcasts while pretending to be on a phone call.

On occasion, I have come close to a respite from loneliness through no fault of my own, and, losing my awareness in a cup of caffeine or the positive interaction of a chance encounter, feel an urgency to engage with my world. Yet, in every instance this eagerness has proved fleeting and has left me to balk at the crucial moment, ultimately reticent to reveal my ignorance of the language or risk making a fool of myself in other ways. The day to day demands on my humility are enough until I find within a person who is willing to be humbled.

One of these moments happened a few weeks ago, when, late at night, like something out of a dream or an incredibly optimistic fairy tale, a beautiful young woman knocked on my door asking to use my Wi-Fi. I was so struck by the impossibility of the moments I initially forgot to say anything at all. The whole encounter felt far too contrived, and it left me speechless. When I did find my voice, no matter what I tried, all it would say is that I did not speak Ukrainian. This was the truth, at the end of the day, but the truth has done little to relieve the biting regret I feel at such a squandered opportunity. I could've at least introduced myself, or inquired as to why she was standing on my threshold, asking to use my internet when the world was asleep like a damsel in a black and white film who had suffered a midnight car crash. To have her explain her situation would've been the least I could do. Instead, I sent her away, desperate to safeguard myself from the possibility of tripping on my words.

The next morning I quickly memorized the Ukrainian for "Please come in, can I get you a glass of wine while you connect to my router?[8]"

I've never used it.

Another such incident where misgiving defeated motivation was the time (intentionally singular) I was able to successfully introduce myself to a peer of Ukrainian descent, a girl from my university-level English club who'd asked me for additional practice. Getting past the niceties, however, did little to allay my anxiety, and when I told her, after a disjointed conversation in a language most aptly described as Ukrainglish, it was healthy to see

---

[8] "Будь ласка, заходьте, чи можу я отримати вам келих вина, поки ви підключаєтеся до мого маршрутизатора?"

her, and after she'd declared I had "the eyes of a cow," I felt my isolating uncertainties very rational, indeed. While I believe both our intentions were to admire the other, these compliments were dramatically lost in translation. At this point, I'm forced to assume she's received all the help she needed elsewhere. She's continued to attend the clubs, but I haven't heard from her since.

Equally frustrating and even more isolating have been my rare encounters with native English speakers who are here unaffiliated with the Peace Corps. Of the two I've met, one was a devout Mormon missionary who wanted little to do with my lack of devotion, the other a young man in Europe after fleeing a felony drug possession charge in Missouri. Without explicitly giving voice to our various concerns, each of us mutually concluded it would be best to stay out of the other's way.

Any respite on my own accord from this social stagnation has been, thus far, unsuccessful. What brief moments of relief I've felt, and I say this with apprehensive awareness of its stark connotation, can be accredited to alcohol.

While my haplessness is less my fault in the case of the other Americans I've encountered, those interactions down to simple bad luck or the pronouncedly foreign, fugitive nature of the country we inexplicably met within, in my daily interactions I have only me to blame. As such, I have occasion to drink when the occasion arises, alcohol impeding my ability to create conscious effect to the effect of taking from myself the chance to get in my own way.

We've talked about alcohol before.

You were exposed to my regrets as I became more removed, greater dissociated from the persona I presented because of the persistent, near-inevitable role of alcohol in the social settings I fell into and the lifestyle to which I was therefore remanded. You witnessed firsthand as it grew to occupy a place of routine, even I never fully accepted this indulgence. In those days, there were moments when I longed for this drastic move, any drastic move. Not change for its own sake, but that the extreme difference in external circumstance might translate to extreme differences in internal ones. I hoped, relying on a childhood of such displacements, that with the chance to start again, far from anyone or anything I'd known before, I could build a life free from who I was, free from this collective compulsion to drink. You were privy to these thoughts. I wonder whether it was any easier to say goodbye, or any harder to admit you loved me, when you knew I'd one day chase that escape I craved. Maybe you hoped I'd let them go, as I hoped when I said I love you.

Regardless, though I am aware, having moved dramatically, that I brought myself with me and that I always will, and though I know I'm not the first or only person to mistakenly associate setting with self and that this desire to refresh the external is attributed to much more than alcohol, when it comes to drinking, and any perceived social reliance on its effects, I am tempted again to leave it all behind, and ignore the preliminary lessons of my time here.

For better or worse, there is no perfectly fresh start, and I am here for two years. Thus, when my host grandmother first offered me a glass of vodka to wash down the chocolates I had brought as a gift, I accepted. I wanted to be a gracious guest, yes, but deep down, I wanted not to say no. I was never very assertive, here or before, and I believe, having unintentionally reflected on it, the root of my issues with alcohol is my struggle as a social chameleon. I drank that night. I drank with my new friends. I drank before my presentation. I drank to fit in, and have done so, often, since settling here.

While it was easy in those early years of self-discovery, the college years, by which they're summarized once they've passed, to blame the alcohol for the choices I made, drugs are nothing but tools with which we liberate ourselves from certain inhibitions. They are instruments, and they require we use them. They do not act separate from ourselves. I have no issue with the nature of alcohol. I never have. All along, I simply found issue with the effect it had on me. Though I found in it the perfect character scapegoat, a silent and ever-familiar excuse upon which to heap the burden of any regrettable behavior, and though thought and guilt, often accompanied by pain, return in force once its effects have worn off, it is not, itself, bad.

This is all a long-winded means by which I hope to justify my reveling in invigorating effects of a stiff pull of Carpathian cognac, in the joys of liberation, in the relief of virile connection communicated between the glossy eyes of two soon-to-be-companions enjoying a drink together. It is impossible to deny how anti-lonely intoxication can be for the optimistic, and here, in a place where alcohol holds such a culturally strong significance, there have been no shortage of its intermittently euphoric experiences.

Beginning with that autobiographical presentation I gave in an accidental stupor, I have shared a drink with many of my fellow villagers. I've visited homes, shared inebriated dinners and stories, and have stifled isolation with every pour. Most prominent in my memory, ironic for how little I remember of the night, was the birthday part of my counterpart. She invited me to the address hours before, conceivably out of compulsion, and I showed up late one evening to the small building a block away from my apartment, where a row of four sauna rooms were hidden by a cross-hatched gate thick with old vines like ropes. In the muggy, wood-paneled room to which I was called to, furthest from the entrance and just past the icy unlit pool, the bottles of vodka outnumbered the guests. We collected ourselves and we toasted her, and everyone, and the country, and our town, and our group. While we celebrated, much like the bread I'd forced down in that office room, I struggled to consume as much of the smorgasbord of appetizers as I could in between shots. Unfortunately, dried anchovies and potato pancakes do very little to absorb the liquor. After we exhausted tradition, I was asked for an American drinking ritual, and in lieu of red solo cups, or a deck of cards, I tried to teach them "Never Have I Ever". In translation, as my first example went like "never have I ever kissed a Ukrainian" (trying to lead the topic to an esoteric place for someone like myself, and buy my liver some time) I somehow communicated this was a game with the goal of naming nationalities we'd never kissed, and, as I was the only one in the room who had travelled outside his own country, I eventually had to pour my shots over my shoulder whenever most of the group was otherwise occupied. Gratefully, the eyes of the room were far from fixed on me, and the steamed liquor hissed quietly under the cacophony of steadily building boisterousness. The scent of vaporized vodka went unnoticed. As the party wore on, ways to maintain consciousness became evermore pressing, and I was the only one who used the pool that night. Eventually, I had to walk home or crash onto the floor. I learned, later, they had continued in the same pace hours after I was fast asleep, and though teased for my abrupt departure, the memory of our shared happiness was enough to stave loneliness for as long as I felt the hangover.

Then, I attended a work event, and learned the truth behind drunken kinship.

An additional illustration of this sottish deliverance from isolation, perhaps a culmination of the sentiment I'm trying to portray, that what is felt in a drink fades and what is replaced by a drink is later felt all the more pronouncedly, occurred at a party held in honor of Ukrainian Local Governments Day.

After generations of Soviet Union occupation, the country had enacted a national holiday, meant to celebrate the recent decentralization of power. Though many throughout the nation had reservations for the policy, everyone, nonetheless, seemed to participate in the revelry.[9] There had been previous events when we gathered and drank at the mayor's restaurant, but this was special. My suit and tie were finally not out of place, and the interior was decorated as ornately as it's guests. The tables were heaped with local delicacies, there was a photo booth with a shining golden backdrop, a glittering DJ stand towered above, we were given signed name cards, and shimmering spotlights and brilliant disco balls replaced the nondescript light fixtures. To complete the effect, the master of ceremonies, a mayoral deputy, had donned a white suit and addressed the crowd all night with a gameshow-esque enthusiasm and vibrato.

What next transpired was so outside my realm of limited experience, the best I can aptly summarize the event would be to

---

[9] As a note, I should make a mentioned that the Ukrainian calendar boasts a dizzying plethora of 'Day's, whether in memoriam or jubilee.

liken it to a local government prom. Names were called, speeches were given, and, most notably to the theme of this letter, toasts were had. There were several dance breaks, some where I was relegated to a circle of older women eager to hold my hand while we pranced around a group of chanting men, and some were more intimate variations, where I swung back and forth and avoided awkward or pitying eye contact. A steady cohort of department heads and local bigwigs, even the odd non-profit owner or police chief, all stood up to toast the occasion. Eventually, my turn to hold the microphone came.

Allow me to preface this by emphasizing two things: 1) You have never heard me sing aloud. There is good reason for this. When I was in boarding school, I tried out for the prestigious "small choir", a group of students as prestigious to our community as a quidditch team to Harry Potter's. When Mr. Rogers, the aptly named choir director, with his wire-rimmed un-ironic spectacles and wispy, demeaning tone, heard my audition, his initial reaction was to ask if I were trying out as a joke. This was even before my voice dropped. 2) There had been several men that night who spoke before me, and most of them had concluded their speeches with a song. These were resonant, rounding ballads, which they led with their booming voices from deep within their socially-compelled beer bellies. The older men on the German side of my family bear these as well, though most had never been taught to make similar use of them. These men had and they sang with incredible gusto, my coworkers joining in and filling the room with their masculine bass. My mind was harkened to the soldiers' drinking halls described in Tolstoy's *War and Peace*. The experience was truly surreal, and inspiring. When my name was called, I climbed the steps to the stage with lingering goosebumps and a stymied performance anxiety.

Had I not been several shots of cognac deep, apprehension would have been much more prevalent, and may have saved me. As it were, however, I confidently approached the stand. Conversation had ceased. Where others had shared the spotlight with food, dance, and the bathroom, the foreigner had the benefit of the doubt, and everyone's attention. With its bated breath the room waited for what I was going to do. When I concluded my prepared remarks, two or three sentences describing my gratitude at having been invited to such a special night, some cheered, not for the virtue of the words, but for the fact I had managed them at all.

Then the mayor told me to sing.

As the suggestion escalated into a chant I had no choice but to appease the crowd, a concession, I'll admit, I was pleased to make. I had too much of my recent history being lonely, and my desperate extroverted tendencies had been teased by the ceremony, and completely unhinged three shots ago. I excused the DJ and typed "Don't Stop Believing instrumental" into his laptop. It was a song I once lip-synced at a 5th grade talent show and was confident I still knew the words to.

Those iconic keys sounded.

I smiled widely, wrapped my hand around the greasy black microphone, and took a deep inhale. Then I yelled my best "Just a small town girl!"

The crowd was, in a word, unresponsive. Yet the melody had started, and there was no going back. Anxious for a reaction, I took the mic from the stand and began to pace the room.

With a few encouragements, I gave my coworkers, my boss, and my purpose for being in the country a passionate, 3 AM dive-bar rendition of the 80's classic. At times I was a full octave below Gregg Rollie's smooth falsetto, at others, I was somewhere in between with my squeaky own. I didn't care. I was drunk, thrilled to be among people, and desperate to show myself to them.

By the time I recognized how badly I'd misread the room I also learned I'd incorrectly assumed this popular American anthem had made its way across the world as I'd seen many of the more current American pop songs had. In the utter lack of any recognition from those previously-intrigued eyes, I knew, beyond applause, my standing as a respected member of the community hung in the balance. In my mind, then, if I hadn't given them something to sing along to, I was going to give them a show, damnit! Embracing the spirit of the era, I shut my eyes, swung my hips, and danced my way around the room, stopping only to point towards the oldest woman at each table, a demographic I could usually rely on, and serenading her with whatever part of the song I was at. The response, was I sober enough to recognize it, developed in steady progressing from confusion, to shock, and finally to horror as I lost myself in the rhythm and my hair swung along with my air guitar solo.

The next day it was explained to me the songs performed before mine were all of a folk variety, of the kind traditionally sung at any national commemoration. They were proud, national anthems, celebrating the country, its people, and their service to the ideals of Ukraine. What the mayor had requested from me was something culturally comparable. "America the Beautiful" would have sufficed, perhaps even "This Land is My Land" (The political misgivings of those particular lyrics would not have been felt by any in the room, but the tone and tune would've been patriotic enough to be appropriate). Journey, while an icon, is not an American foundation, and the Mick Jagger moves I incorporated into my performance were seen as wholly poor taste.

I was not invited to the after party, and you can surmise how this gaff has since heightened my isolation.

With all this said, I am loath to find a conclusion. What seems fitting does not seem uplifting, and, if possible, considering the tone I've set of my time away thus far, I'd rather avoid leaving you again in melancholy.

Instead of a tonally suitable ending, I could implore you "Don't EVER stop believing you can sing well enough to do karaoke", or might say, to no effect, "Don't EVER stop believing that every experience is what you make it." Something that might bring a smile, words which lend to the peaceful notion that my absence is worth our separation in the incalculable value of the experiences I have enjoyed since I arrived. Unfortunately, neither ending is where I am right now.

In this letter, in my mind, I am lonely.

Notwithstanding this confession, the English teacher living rent-free in my mind demands I infer something, some summary of these meandering pages. So I'll tell you that it is with my own nature, the self, exposed in the elation, where I find fault. Not with the isolation, not with the alcohol, but with the person who has been revealed in all of it. It is within, that I need to work, and without, that I need to accept.

Lastly, because you once told me you thought postscripts were the equivalent of cheating on a narrative, I write here my hope that the journey on which I send these words will lend them some sense, that in this envelope they will age like wine in its cask. I hope they, are at the very least, digestible once they've reached your mailbox. If this is not the case, I promise to send more soon.

Wistfully,

Sam

6.

"Part of the work of being a modern person seems to be dreaming of alternative lives in which you don't have to dream of alternate lives. We long to stop longing, but we also wring purpose from that desire"

Joshua Rothman

Dear Michelle,

Your reply was correct, and thank you for reminding me I have yet to tell you about my work here.

In my defense, this being I think the sixth time I'm writing you, there are certainly more than five things worth examining about a life before its profession. My Ukrainian colleagues have solidified this perspective; many have often told me how strange it is that we in America, or perhaps, the "West," make use of our work title or job description to self-describe. It's a fair point. What does analyst, or, for that matter, volunteer, really say about me?

Though, I admit, since work is the primary purpose of my being here, and since I've more than touched upon other aspects of my experience, I suppose it's past time for me to broach the subject.

To preface with an observation, though.

If I may.

Again, your response was correct, and quite damning. I do tend to lose myself, and so the pull of unity, in writing. Without the ability to reread what I've sent you I have to concede to your admonishment, an incoherence in the overarching image of my existence in this place does not require an incoherence in the individual letters themselves. Yet I wouldn't be myself in them if I didn't hazard the occasional self-indulgent, meta, and often, to be fair, fairly apparent observation about society, conclusions anyone with the time to think about these things to even a fraction of the extent I presently enjoy might come to.

Hypothetical thought is a privilege, certainly. Not only do I have time to consider life, but I am also aware of seemingly infinite considerations with which to do so. Had I more pressing concerns, a narrower realm of possibility, these lenses, the retrospective perspectives, hindsight from the ends of each of my uncertain paths, would be much more specific. I have reservations about contributing to the modern West's prosperity of dilletante philosophers, but what else am I to do with opportunity to think, the chance to live nearly any life I want? The best way I can see to escape the pitfalls of complacency, to avoid the mortal sin of privilege, which is to squander my advantages, is to use my time to understand the world and those within it, and, only then, decide how to best live for it, and for them.

In this vein, thank you for humoring my musings, especially if they are inferences you've already reached. If there is as little merit to them as I sometimes suspect, please keep me from further intellectual self-pleasuring and demand future communiqués be more descriptive than prescriptive.

Until such time, however, before I tell you about work, I have an observation about it.

We (those who comprise my peer group, my generation, and, sometimes, I believe most modern human beings) work to travel.[10] We work to travel, in that we earn money enough to save, and when we have saved enough we take a trip. On these trips, we travel to see places where other people work, working to travel to where we've come from, and where we work. On this carousel, we swap places for a week, and then, once we've exhausted the reason for our labor for the fruits of theirs, we return, and work to earn enough to swap with someone else. The most devastatingly ironic thing about it all is that we believe life is different in the places we are going to. We cling to this notion despite every capability of our

---

[10] Some of us volunteer to travel instead, but to similar effect.

online consciousness to disprove it. If we took the time to search somewhere new, we would diminish our desire to see it, as the more we know about a place the less there is to discover, and, online, we can know almost everything about everywhere.

The question I'm faced with, as I observe myself under this thought experiment, as I work through the two years I've pledged, in what amounts to a work while travelling agreement, is the work, and the travel I receive as compensation, worth it? I understand that by asking this question I will have immortalized myself in your mind as a half-baked societal critic, who will forever hypocritically fawn for the most prosaic forms of mental numbing (are you caught up with Game of Thrones yet?). Still, it feels interesting enough to fill a page or two, and so, is it worth it? To work eleven, and the better part of a twelfth, months to see some different buildings, hear a different language, and eat different foods for a few days?

On average, it appears by behavior that our collective answer is a resounding "yes". Of course it's a yes, my peers scream at me, your pompous ass has smiled on that Disneyland ride as well as the millions before you. My withdrawn contemplation has left save my approximation of the public to curb any haughtiness. But, if I ignore their imagined reproach, if we all took a step back, if we allowed ourselves the crippling possibility that most of what we do is objectively foolish, are these experiences ever distinct enough to impart the relief we crave from the commonplace? Whether I'm in Brussels or Denver, the complexities of life which make mundane the mundane still exists. In the mood of those millions who return to work and immediately begin preparations for their next trip, the answer to my question should be "not really". Yet, meek and aware or proud and unconcerned, we bookmark Expedia all the same.

Isn't that absurd?

I think this comment, slightly embarrassing because the realization has dawned upon me fairly early into the two years I gave myself to realize it, is why I've been so hesitant to tell you about my work here.

If I explained to you that, at its core, my work is well and truly same as it would be if I were working in a local government in the States, privy to the same underlying bureaucracy and pervasive boredom amplified by tedious tasks, the key distinctions being the peculiarities of buildings we work, the language we use to work, and the food which sustains our efforts, wouldn't that make you incredibly sad I ever forced us to say goodbye to each other? Logically, if this were the case, the only purpose for this painful separation was so that I could discover my ignorance of myself firsthand. It's an unpleasant conclusion and I've refrained from dwelling upon it. I haven't talked about work because of the inherent ordinariness of such a conversation. I haven't told you about work because I worried your familiarity with what I would say might lead you to wonder why I bothered to come here. I haven't told you about the days of grinding out the hours in pretend engagement, learning Python on YouTube until the relief of a lunch break, about the myriad grant applications I've written that will never win funding because I'm not allowed to submit them and my immediate organization willfully ignores the constraints of my larger responsibilities to the Peace Corps, or that my elementary school English club is often the one concrete task I complete each week. Patterns make for terrible stories, and even more so when the patterns I fled from, and caused us so much pain to do so, are here, too.

Then, a few nights ago, from the depths of this barren well, an outwardly commonplace event became a quintessential moment of my Ukrainian experience, and I finally had work worth telling you about.

Or, as it may come to be known if I can tell it right, the story of:

Three Men and a Broom:
How a Disaster of a Project Became My Reckoning with the Joys of Daily Life

* * *

It was a late afternoon on the fourth floor. My counterpart and I were in the city of Uzhhorod, a picturesque European capital located equidistant from the borders of Hungary and Slovakia and an oftentimes harrowing 40 minute bus ride from our village.

The building whose top floor we sat in belonged to a non-profit whose name translated roughly to "Develop Zakarpattia", Zakarpattia being our shared rayon of Ukraine. This organization were hosting us and several other representatives from surrounding city councils as part of a two-day workshop on local government work, one of those training initiatives which international funding groups love to see on paper but would be loath to attend in actuality. Having previously been exposed to a few similar proceedings, conducting one of my own at the conclusion of my training, I can say with confidence that, more often than not, what the attendees went home with were a stack of highly-optimistic pamphlets, a free pen or two or a branded tote bag, the few statistics which managed to stick in their minds with varying degrees of future practicality, and an ebbing caffeine high from the quintessential and complimentary espresso. Granted, there was probably much more to be gotten out of the presentations if one spoke the language, but even if I understood any of it, I believe my pronouncement would still hold true, on average. These trainings were a deliverable, a line on a budget, an attractive paragraph on an application. They were, to say it in fewer words, generally more for the sake of the speaker than for to whom he/she speaks.

I'll spare you the names of the day's attendants. In all honestly, I only retained the ones of those in my breakout group, and only then because I had plenty of time to repeat them to myself while they worked on a poster presentation due in ten minutes, a collection of bubble-lettered words underneath a heading I believe meant: "Difficulties of Local Government Cooperation." I surmised the interpretation from the bullet point "unwilling to change."

When we weren't building lists, or working on how to present our small group presentations to the others present at the presentation, most of what was said passed directly over my head, so, for the better part of two days, I busied myself in other observations and anxiety over whether I'd sat straight enough to appear engaged when the camerawoman came into the room at the top of every hour.

Gratefully, from my seat in the painfully whitewashed room, where the colorless floors and walls and ceiling and desks were all meant to give an impression of new, modern, and which rendered the space soulless, I could just make out the banks of the quaint European river which lolled through the center of town. Like Cameron and his movie-magic moment with the Georges Seurat painting, I engrossed myself in the goings-on of the river's visitors for as long as the training photographer allowed. This woman, an employee of the non-profit, would, without warning, suddenly enter the room several times throughout the day. Her camera snapped the room into apt attention because we had seen she wasted no time in the immediate documenting of the day's attendants. All of us understood the pictures were, ultimately, what we'd come for, whether they were to be used as proof of the training's occurrence and our attendance or to supplement the respective Facebook posts sure to be posted by the pages of every organization represented in the room soon after they'd left. None of us, especially the foreign-looking individual highlighted by the dazed gloss over his eyes and the not-yet-fully-assimilated attire which was sure to be a focus of the group photos, wanted to appear apathetic.

While the photographer stood, then, and for a brief period after she returned to her office, I would glue my gaze to the slideshow, retaining nothing. My attention, when it was no longer distracted with appearances, reverted immediately outside, and to the night's deadline.

The grant application for my first project, proposed to appease my mayor and not for any semblance of practicality, was due in five hours, and there were days' worth of tasks I needed to finish before I could submit it.

I knew, as the clock ticked as the background noise to a collective complaint against the holdovers of Soviet-era local government which had proven resilient to everyone in the room, we would never win the funding. There were too many loose ends, too many hypotheticals I was forced to present as assurances, but I had to make a good faith effort, or be singularly ridiculed at the next Monday staff meeting.

After lunch, a pleasant spread of Hungarian cuisine and copious coffee and cake, we resumed for the final presentation, and I began calculating the minimum time I would need to at least fill every textbox on the Swiss government website with the required characters and a passable Ukrainian translation.

The deduction, no matter how much I shaved off reality, did not bode well.

During the bathroom break, I explained this to my counterpart. The day of training, an event I hadn't anticipated because I'd been unaware I would be attending until the morning when I was handed a bus ticket and told to follow my counterpart to the station, had upended my schedule, and, even if we returned to the office immediately after getting home, I told her I might not be able to finish writing the grant.

She was unconvinced. I think the proposal, to build a technology center in city hall, was her idea before it was passed down from the mayor through her, but she never took credit for it. It was her job to voice the wishes of her superiors, not to claim credit for them, and it was mine to communicate to the Swedish government that ideas she passed along were achievable. In this case, that the empty office space above the second-floor bathroom could exist as a place where village residents would come and work on the free computers, attend youth development trainings, and develop their entrepreneurial tendencies, and would not exist solely so that the city council could have a lovely new whitewashed space of their own, the hotel across the street being less than a long-term solution which had long since regretted granting the city council cart-blanche permission to host its presentations inside. Especially, I imagined, after the mess I made of mine.

Ever the optimist, my counterpart promptly set off to find a solution. I returned to the conference room to learn she'd elicited the help of a good friend of hers, a young local volunteer and activist who'd, in the spirit of this country I'd discovered to this point, unreservedly agreed to help me translate the application materials.

Given the eight hour hell I was about to put him through, it may surprise you to know we've become good friends, and I'll often stop for coffee with him on my way to the university English clubs whenever I'm in his city.

Once the workshop was over, concluding with an entreaty to follow the host organization's social media page and invitations to attend next month's conference on farming co-ops regardless of our agricultural engagement, my new project partner and I were provided an empty office space in the room adjacent the conference hall, a laptop, and unlimited access to the espresso machine.

By the end of the day, I had consumed nine of them.

The details of our cooperation were, even as I sit here and try to embellish them, tedious. We spent the rest of the afternoon, the evening, and most of the night writing an application as complete strangers planted precariously on the shaky bridge which spanned our cultural divide. One of the more proactive members of "Develop Zakarpattia" would check in on us, and offered input whenever we came across a misinterpretation, including a budget proposal that nearly sent the two of us careening into the depthless fathoms of misunderstanding. The work was slow, the required information dull, made more so in of efforts we had to make to contact the several outside sources who ought to have been in on the project proposal, including a very put out Uzhhorodian desktop distributor and a frustrated single mother long home from the office. Fortunately, these hours are not what make this story.

This was the surprise ending, a not-so-Shyamalan surprise which made me feel the prologue was worth telling. To be clear it's no *Sixth Sense*, but this is a work story, and it's as good as any of those are ever likely to get.

We wrapped up around 11:00 PM (22: 53 as my phone read, since I'd finally changed it to the 24 hour clock used in Europe, much to the future chagrin of friends and family), seven minutes before the call for applications closed. At the time I refused to consider what a last second submission meant for our chances. I was simply jubilant to have met the deadline in the first place.

My weary friend and I shared a smile and a forced high-five, then quickly tidied up the office. When we exited the room, we were shocked to find the "Develop Zakarpattia" representative waiting patiently in the hallway, busying himself with something or other on his phone. Apparently, he had the key we needed to exit the building and couldn't leave without us without locking us in for the night.

I offered a profuse apology which he quickly waived off. We had written a project; this was worth celebrating, he exclaimed, and placed himself between us. With a hearty slap on either shoulder, he cheerfully navigated us into the breakroom.

There, alongside the half-empty package of coffee grounds and a few leftover snacks were a half-full bottle of vodka and three shot glasses, one of which looked to have been put to recent use. We were promptly poured a healthy swig each, and raised our glasses in toast to the day's week of work.

Had I had time to unwind from the grant-writing sprint, I may have remembered I hadn't eaten anything since noon, and that with the last bus to my village leaving in less than 30 minutes, I ought to have politely declined. But I finally had a professional incentive to celebrate, and I happily took all four toasts that were offered. We soon finished the bottle.

The alcohol may soften the disbelief of what happened next, but without telling you we were inebriated you'd be obliged, at the following, to hold us as utter idiots.

Stumbling to the office's front door, making quite a ruckus in the tight, echoing hallway, pitch black but for the neon red of the exit sign, our guide failed to notice the sound of his keys falling from his pocket to the floor. Instead, he held open the heavy, self-locking door for his guests, unaware that the means by which we could leave the building's front door were no longer on his person. He waited for it to slam shut, made sure it was locked, and joined our slow descent down the dark stairwell. When we arrived on the first floor, myself and my new coworker let him step in front of us, watched him pat himself down, and laughingly realize he was no longer in possession of his keys.

Our first reaction was to laugh with him, until my partner translated: "We can sleep on the couch in the office", and then, a few seconds later, "we can't get back inside the office, either."

We were trapped.

To make this more interesting, I've come up with a little choose your own adventure, because I need to be confident that what we did next was our best course of action.

I'll describe the three answers we came up with in the moment, and then let you decide what you would do in our shoes before I tell you what actually transpired. I look forward to reading the same decision we went with.

1) You stay in the building. One of you was sufficiently inebriated to find the cold, stone floor comfortable enough for a night. The others could make do with the jacket, backpack, and paper towels from the first floor restroom. Each of you would have your own personal landing, and you can call your respective bosses in the morning to explain why you'd be late for work.

2) You don't stay in the building. You can't stay in the building. There's just no way you'll accept that as a solution. Are any of the windows capable of being jumped out of? Not if you want to land intact. Are there any other exits? No. Can you call emergency services? This does not warrant an emergency. Can you call anyone else? Everyone else is sleeping, it would be rude to wake them unless it was an emergency. Can you get out? Where would you go? The last bus for Perechyn leaves before you could get there. You could run? It wouldn't help, where would you go? Don't worry, this kind of thing happens all the time, you might as well get used to it and have fun with the new experience, and likely end up with the same sleeping situation as option 1, but with a more complete acceptance of the absurdity of it all and a better attitude to use in future predicaments.

3) You find a way out. You display a little buzzed ingenuity and play your own version of Saw. Or Saw II. Or Saw III. You've never seen any of them, the movies never made it big enough in Ukraine to warrant a place on any Russian pirating websites. But you know of the premise colloquially, and you imagine at least one involves an escape from a locked room. From there, you can learn from your friend the best place to hitchhike if you are to head north back to Perechyn.

What path do you choose?

——————————— Spoilers Below: ———————-

In reality, we went with option #3, though it took convincing for our host not to pass out on the floor.

This required no small inventiveness, and some serious finagling, involving raiding the unlocked second floor offices for a couch, and, fortuitously, a shovel. Leaving a note promising to return both in the morning. Carrying said couch down to the first floor and scratching a number of scuff marks into the walls which I would be unaware of until I returned a week later for the farming training. Climbing on top of the couch and using the shovel to hold the tiny windowpane above the door open long enough for two of us to climb to and crawl through. Tossing the shovel blindly into the street. Using the shovel to pry open the window from the outside while the third member of our group climbed through. Shouting in wild and ecstatic hilarity upon our success, as the American squeezed his torso over the precipice and landed awkwardly on his ass. Lastly, learning how to hitchhike, but, as the practice is rightfully banned by the Peace Corps, I'll withhold these details until the statute of limitations runs.

* * *

Cheers if you guessed correctly, and my kudos if you came up with your own, more level-headed, conclusion.

Either way, there you have as close to a worthily-shareable work story as I've yet to experience. I hope it affords a slightly better understanding of what my job as a volunteer comprises, and a better picture of the people I'm lucky enough to work with. I promise you, it is every bit as confusing, stressful, irritating, demanding, and wonderful as the story implies.

In general, despite the engaging qualities of my overarching role, I feel the need to reiterate, as you've probably surmised in the introductory pages to this story or as I may've mentioned in a previous letter, I have not had much success in day to day responsibilities. Monotony, especially when paired with repeatedly-frustrated initiative, has proved exhausting.

I expect this will work itself out over the years, but in this norming period, I've struggled to cope.

In the meantime, I leave for a holiday trip to L'viv next week. I'm beyond excited to be amongst other Americans again, and I'm hoping the time with these volunteers will rejuvenate, inspire, and, at the very least, be expressly cathartic. Who make better therapists than coworkers you can be yourself with?

I trust, then, my next letter will be far livelier. Until then, please feel free to tell me more about your work and your own, much more budding, career. As you've seen, anything is worth sharing.

Freed,

Sam

7.

"The only people who see the whole picture are the ones who step outside the frame"

Salman Rushdie

Dear Michelle,

A few nights ago, I danced the year away in an utterly beautiful scene.

Before the L'viv Opera with its timeless edifice as grand as any storied, baroque European venue, upon which is projected a laser overlay of Christmas-themed concert displays, the bright neon dancing with the DJ on the balcony and shimmering brilliantly on the polished marble backdrop, is a square as old as the building itself. Surrounding, throughout the holiday season, is a quaint Christmas market, a bustling collection of temporary shacks with untreated wooden facades, constructed to model traditional village homes, and filled with hand-made gifts, food, and drink all served with homemade merriment. The space these stands enclose is heavy with mulled wine and with roasted sausage and grilled mushrooms and fresh popcorn and the crowd is blanketed by the familiar fragrance of cheer. This scent and the sounds and the lights and the smiles which it accompanies are warm, the cold forgotten as one passes underneath one of the wreathed arches which adorn walkway entrances. In the center of this festive cobblestone city block is a massive fountain, resplendent when the water line is connected and, most recently, a makeshift platform of historical significance, a roped-off receptacle of mud, spilt liquor, and the footprints of jubilant, defiant youth.

Some were mine, some other Peace Corps volunteers, some were the Ukrainian teens who first scrambled under the ropes and atop the massive structure, when the countdown concluded and the night transitioned from a New Year's Eve party to a New Year's early morning rave, and some of these muddled footsteps were those others who joined us in the fountain's bowl when the crowd reached a fervor and all anyone wanted to do was to dance, cheer, share a plastic water bottle filled with what tasted like cherry vodka, and be seen.

The night was a revelry, a culmination of carefree abandon only achievable with people you trust, love, and, often, have not seen for some time. With the city a collective carnival, when the Near Year was dawning and the cold low clouds confined the bliss and reflected the pulsing color, when people shouted from balconies at the shouting people in the streets and the shouting was merry, who could blame us? We were trespassing, but we were infinite.

What our fellow celebrants didn't know is that we, the volunteers, had no need for the occasion. This was how we always affected one another. Like teenagers in a stern school or children of strict parents, our semblances of wanton indulgence were seized upon with a sense of near-euphoric relief whenever we were together. A reunion became a celebration became a Saturnalia.

Yet I ask, again, who could blame us?

We were all in our daily worlds so isolated, so outside of any normalcy, so desperate for a feeling of comfort that there grew this tendency to abuse what little we could find. Though this was our own first reconvening since our drastic separation, which brought some solace or, at least, mitigated some regret as we awoke later that day, January 1st, and surveyed in horror the soiled shoes and missing personal items and less than pleasant headspaces, ours was not an isolated experience. Volunteers who'd come before us had related stories of their own reunions, the profound force of collision between friends who, after three months of intensive relationship forming, norming and reliance and after being spread across a country, separated in an instant, came back together with an energy like a star collapsing in on itself. This effect was storied, simply put, it was usually how volunteers affected one another.

What was left in an awareness of this pattern was to embrace the vivacity, smile often, recapture the vigor for service for and from each other, and hope what you lived was enough to get you through the severance until the next time you'd all be together. Following the advice of the cohorts before ours, this is what we did.

I enjoyed every frantic moment of it. I was among friends and felt like myself for the first time in what felt like years.

By the end of the week, however, the frenzy had waned. Despite the days of joy I found my thoughts, invariably, pulled homeward. Initially, I tried hard not to admit them. How could I want to return to my village considering how urgently and recently I'd wanted to be anywhere else?

Still, in the moments of pause, I sensed my mind drawn to the fantasies of falling asleep because there was nothing interesting left to watch, or eating the same dish as the day before because it was all that the shop had, the shop which didn't make me say anything to buy anything. I wondered, then, and as well along my returning train ride, are some vacations simply a time so chaotic and unfamiliar, enough to make you appreciate what you'd be returning to? Are the airports schedules and strange public transports and variable meal times and intense itineraries all to occupy the mind to the point it may reconsider monotony as stability?

Word choice is essential, even more so mentally.

That life can be interchangeably monotonous and stable is nothing more than internalized semantics.

By the end of the week I felt much like Samwise missing the Shire: I'd had enough of adventure, as had most everyone else in the group. Thus, on our last night in the city, after another full day of exploration, the volunteers and I who'd split a hotel room opted to remain there, and we retired to four adjacent twin beds hours earlier than we had the entire trip.

Unfortunately, our internal clocks had been smashed the second day of our Lvivian spree, and this sudden, well-intentioned behavioral change did not inspire a physical one, and our pragmatic approach to a good night's rest amounted to restlessness.

Minutes passed as hours, and as the fruitlessness of our stasis mounted so too did the rustling of blankets. The accidental noises of a post-adolescent human adopted an irritated tone. Grunts became grumpy, maneuverings became manic and tossing became tumultuous, until, at last, one of us shattered the frail silence.

What resulted, as best I can aesthetically title it, was:

An Adult Sleepover in L'viv.

A story like a sister-child to An American in Paris, *with the same jobless protagonists and in a similarly-foreign city, but absent the mutual love interest and taking place entirely in a dark room where all the dialogue was directed at, and spoken into, the void.*

"I can't sleep", bed #2 said.[11]

#4 concurred.

"I'm glad you said something," I said. "I'm getting nowhere over here."

"So… what do we do now?", queried #2 or #4.

"Shut up and keep trying," #3 groaned. He went on to contribute little to the conversation and preserved the American in Paris formula of three leading men.

"You guys think he's still mad about last night?", #4 verbally winked, in reference to #3's week-long and ultimately hapless effort to find love in a foreign place.

"I would be too if I was out 1000 hryvnia.[12]"

"I've lost a lot more than that this weekend, if that's what he's upset about."

#3 impolitely suggested the others go ahead and leave him out of the rest of the conversation, if a conversation was what was to ensue. Ironically, his outburst, muttered with sufficient annoyance

---

[11] For the sake of anonymity, the volunteers will be referred to by their bed's position in the room, in sequence starting from whoever's was nearest the bathroom door. Mine was first.

[12] Ukrainian local currency. The exchange rate at the time of these events was 27 UAH for every 1 dollar, so #3 was out no small sum for a heartbroken volunteer

to elicit laughter, all but ensured the others were now fully awake. The pace of whispers increased accordingly, and yet, once his name stopped coming up, #3's efforts to doze off seemed to have met much more success. That, or his patience grew three sizes that day. This was the last we heard from his position within the darkness.

When the muffled laughter and slew of teasing subsided, I asked the ceiling, "You guys ever feel trapped in your sites?"

A pause.

"What do you mean?", #2 replied, in a tone which betrayed he might know exactly the sentiment I'd alluded to.

I expanded all the same.

"I guess, I don't know. Ever since I moved out of my host family's house, since I got my own place and finally made the last move I'll make for the next two years, I've felt, cooped up. I don't know. Like, mentally, constipated."

"Mentally WHAT?"

"You know what I mean. I'm sure you know what I mean. Like, since I got here, since we got here, we've been running everywhere. We've been placed everywhere, from training to transition to our sites, and it felt like we were always moving, or working towards the next move. Now, I can't really stop. I can't ignore the momentum. I want to keep running. Except now, with nowhere to go, no something else to expect, it's almost like the only recourse I have left is to run from, instead of to. Almost as if I need to regret something because I can't look forward to something."

Another pause.

"I know what you mean about the expecting something else," said #2. "It's hard for me to trust a routine in this place. It's been hard to settle as well.

But I think it's more I don't trust myself not to mess something up outside of my apartment."

I smiled; no one saw.

"Exactly!", I almost shouted. "Like I go to the same fucking store every time I need something because it's the only one that doesn't make me speak any Ukrainian when I checkout."

"Oh yeah, I've avoided the bazaar in my village like the plague."

"Why?"

"No electronic checkout."

"What about you, [#4]?"

I could hear him weigh the question, and I pictured him pondering like an impassive Egyptian sarcophagus, his hands on his chest, resting in thought. #4 was older than the rest of us, and, for as long as I'd known him, was effortlessly charismatic and unimpeachably self-assured. I often wondered, given how I imagined he'd find success wherever he went in life, why he'd come to Ukraine at all. The rest of us, after we'd been able to get to know one another, all possessed some sort of glaring character flaw or obvious unresolved crisis we'd come to sort out. He was simply there. Though often the source of mischief and amusement in the group, and though we never admitted or agreed to this, we all held him like an older brother, the unspoken leader archetype in any group dynamic, incapable of insecurity.

Or, at least, it seemed that way.

"I think when I stopped caring about my pronunciation was when I started to really embrace this experience," he said, authentically, and without the tacit pretension such a comment might be imbued with if either of us said anything similar.

#2, apparently too tired to concern himself with the understated intent of this comment, chuckled. "Your Ukrainian is pretty shit."

"I wish I could get rid of my self-consciousness."

"It's not like I'm not self-consciousness," #4 reassured me.

"How'd you stop caring, then?"

"I fucked up."

"Wouldn't that make it worse?"

Before we could continue our sidebar, #2, eager to keep the banter universally relevant, mentioned a name we hadn't discussed since training.

"You guys hear [x] dropped out?"

"Yeah, [y] texted me about it a few days ago.

"Wait, actually?"

"Yeah, he went home last week."

"Did [x's girlfriend, the second half of one of the most eventful, toxic, and gossip-worthy relationships I'd ever been aware of in reality] leave with him?"

"You didn't hear? She was gone like a month ago."

"And apparently they'd started talking again ever since."

"Jesus."

"So what is that now, seven?"

"Times they got back together?"

"Including [z]?"

"I'm not."

"[z] counts."

"He was literally sent home the day after we flew in."

"What'd he do again?"

"Blacked out and pissed himself after breaking like half the lobby."

"Still arrived with us though."

"I don't want to count him. Eight feels like a lot."

"I don't know. Seven is still high for a first-year cohort, apparently."

"Where do you guys think [x] is?"

"Guarantee you he's back in Seattle. It's all he ever talked about."

"Probably."

As often happens with light, late night hearsay, each of us wordlessly lingered on one another's decision; under the guise of absorbing new information, we applied our own perspective to the choices our peers had made, choices we sometimes wished we'd make.

Every time another volunteer returned to the States I found it easier and harder to stay.

"You think he's happier?"

"[x]?"

"Definitely not [x's girlfriend, now a key player in the Northwestern pyramid scheme market]."

"I don't know man. Was he ever happy here?"

"He was always so worried about getting sent home."

"What, why?"

"I never heard that."

"He was in my language group. He always thought his language wasn't up to par, no matter how many times we told him the assessment didn't matter."

"Little did he know."

"For real, they'll take whoever they can get."

"But they make a good show of it until you find that out."

"That illusion crashed pretty quickly when I couldn't even remember black and white."

"Why'd they ask you about colors?"

"I told them I liked to play chess."

"You hate chess."

"Yeah, but it's an easy word to remember."

"*Shach-hey.*"

"That's so weird though," I let slip, bringing us back to our most recently-fallen comrade.

"Why?"

"I guess I just felt like if he was anxious about staying, he was happy to be here. He was the last person I thought would go home on his own volition."

"Just say choice, you dick."

"Maybe he was just an anxious person."

"Do you think he regrets it?"

A significantly heavier pause.

Of course, this last question was the reason we were all bundled in this drafty hotel room with what amounted to a prison shower next door, its sickly green décor hiding the certain mold, opening to a dusty hallway in a forgotten corner of this ancient city well beyond its golden age.

#4 was the first to speak, but the depth of the question had appropriated the spirit of the conversation, and though we continued, sleep came soon for the self-reflecting minds.

"I can't help thinking it would have been so much healthier if we could decide when our time here was over," he surmised, softly, while #2 and I reflected. "We all came to satisfy some itch, I think. But for me, and I think for most of us, we quickly found that some were easier to scratch than others. A few of us imposed their will on the two years and left right away, discovering this experience would not be molded to fit any expectation. And an even fewer of us were ready to accept whatever came, because they brought with them what the rest of us came for.

"Or they found it early on," I said, dreamily.

"Yeah, probably."

I waited for #2 to say something, but it seemed somewhere in #4's slow rumination his own had given way to dreams.

Two of four remained.

"I think I was definitely someone who came to 'get something out of my system', you know, before I finally acquiesced to a normal life.

As the stereotype goes."

"Have you?", he asked me.

"I don't know."

"Will you?"

"I fucking hope so."

Thus the conversation ebbed. Somewhere, a siren swelled. The wretched little heater bravely droned. We slept.

In the morning, we said goodbye at the train station.

The new year had begun.

* * *

I'll admit to you, Michelle, what I couldn't tell #4, or any of the others, that night.

I have not found what I came for. I knew that as clearly as I know it now. I haven't gotten anything out of my system. I haven't scratched the itch. All I've done is focus my attention solely on the act of itching even if I've yet to find what needs to be scratched. Focusing on the itch, I feel them all over.

I came here for me.

As such, I am bound to fail.

That, I didn't know quite yet. While I rode my way back to the village, I clung to the blind optimism of adjustment, still hoping I'd find, in time, what I came for.

We are the same person on either side of midnight, even on January 1st.

* * *

The first vacation from a new home is often a pivotal one. Coming back can make somewhere feel familiar more than living there ever did. Returning to a place imbues it with a sense of recognition, a comfort that may go unrecognized until you have left, and come back.

When I saw my village come around the mountain bend, its quaintness from a distance, the cracks in the walls and pavement more apparent as we drew near and the train slowed, I saw my life here with the perspective lent me by my holiday. I saw what it was really like, for a moment, what life was in an objective sense, when I wasn't absorbed in the newness of it all.

I saw what almost felt like home.

I watched myself climb one of the residential hills on the outskirts of town, green from a distance, following the obscure route Google Maps was taking me to secure the package my parents had sent, with things I missed most from the States. What I and the available data on the town of Perechyn thought was the address of the post office was, in fact, the home of the local delivery driver. After summiting this hill in the late afternoon, I watched a group of nervous children stare at the tall, smiling, and strangely confident foreigner who had knocked on their door while both their parents were still at work, and who, in a broken version of their language, inquired about his belongings while shooing their pet goat and a few of the more assuming chickens who roamed the yard. I felt my palms were sweaty, as they had been when one of the shirtless self-babysat children started crying after I'd raised my voiced to enunciate my paltry vocabulary, his wailing shattering any remaining illusion that my app had led me to the correct location. As the train cars leaned from a turn, I recalled dashing from their threshold, past the farm animals and overturned tricycle, back through the gate and down the muddy hill in my nicest pair of dress shoes, drawing dismissive, puzzled looks from every concerned housewife within sight of my folly. I'd learned, then, perhaps my overreliance on online directions had been unfounded.

Not my best moment.

The house near the train station, there where the pavement gave way to gravel, was where we, my counterpart, some of her friends, and I, had concluded our Christmas caroling. Blind drunk from the shots of vodka we were all encouraged to enjoy, the cookies and candies offered alongside doing little to offset the effects, at each of the several homes we visited once we'd concluded our contrite rendition of the two or three Ukrainian folk songs rehearsed on the walk over, I, for obvious reasons, hadn't retained much of real significance in my memory of that night. Yet, now, my feet making tracks in the snow in a much more uniform manner, and drinking the chill with gratitude, free of the airless cabin, rather than the resentment I'd felt at being drug outside to yet another household, I strode past the silent porch and looked in through the curtained windows and witnessed the eagerness with which I'd consumed the oranges in the hand painted porcelain bowl, hoping their juice would sober me more effectively than water. As I watched a figure step past the light, I recalled with horror and humor the spectacle I must have been as I stumbled to the safety of my apartment, which, because I'd bought groceries before the holidays, I don't think I left again for at least 72 hours.

Past the station, I was walking into town as I'd done nearly every day since my initial arrival. The sky was a wintry morning grey, the streets oppressively silent, and the echo of the crunching snow forcing reflection on the snapshots preserved along the way. I remembered the time I'd invited another volunteer to help give a presentation on small businesses to my office, and my look of bemused satisfaction at the look of absolute horror which swept across his face when he received that potent whiff of rubbing alcohol factory runoff which braced me every morning.

I was reminded then, and now, with a fresh nose from a week away, how truly pungent the scent was.

I saw myself walking into the small park at the center of the village, more a large patch of grass and brush and trees with a statue centered within, currently whitewashed by a fresh mountain flurry, to meet a man whom my counterpart had taken ski lessons from. She'd encouraged me to meet with him in case I ever had the budget to do the same and to see if I could convince him to attend one of my youth clubs and provide free lessons to the kids. I observed, the quiet chill stealing the sense of general apprehension I'd felt at the time, the actual event of my addressing an individual with the white coat I was told to look for. Although he was not the person I was supposed to meet and had simply been sporting a similar sense of fashion, this individual went along with my practiced greeting without a moment's hesitation and nearly convinced me to loan him 500 hryvnia before the man I'd written the introduction for noticed our interaction from across an empty chair at the adjacent café and stepped between us in the nick of time. I felt an amazement at the first person's flexibility of purpose, taking in stride that he was, without his knowledge, a ski instructor I'd been instructed to meet and immediately adapting this newfound purpose into his original intent to ask me for money.

This admiration replaced the embarrassment which had overwhelmed all else at the time.

Outside of town and much to my own chagrin, when I strolled past one of the several lots of overgrowth which neighbored my rural building, in my mind's eye I again was unwilling witness to the shocking image of what I can best describe as a stray dog cuckhold situation which greeted, or rather, assaulted, me the morning of my first Friday with the city council.

If only I could tell you all the memories I owed to these village walks.

Finally, as I turned onto the sodden street which bordered my apartment, I recognized, with the lens of being away, a fondness for what most resembled a home in my present experience, that that living in Ukraine, living in a village, living somewhere that greets you on a cold, dark morning with an impossibly impassive stillness, is an extended reflection on mortality.

One long contemplation of life at its every stage, from its most simple, and happy, to its most grim, and fundamental.

This village, my home, was a genuine microcosm of existence. Preserved from the ever-complicated sense of life that is demanded by the developed world, protected from modern society's muddling of purpose.

Purpose, that is, if you're able to see it, ultimately simple. Like the village. What you see is what you get, and what I saw is what there was. Birth, life, and death, with work, family, tasks trivial and consequential, thrown in between. Life is to live.

What you see is what you get. The maxim which might be an answer to all philosophy.

Consider another adage.

Have you ever heard the tale of the dirty car? Did you parents ever explain to you that a dirty car gets dirtier, while a clean car tends to stay clean? (In my case, my mom often used this as a metaphor for the state of my eternal soul, how sin builds upon itself while a cleaned conscious has a predisposition to stay clean because it has yet to allow any new blemishes. But I wonder if yours imparted the proverb without the intense spiritual implications.)

With my fresh perspective, I speculate whether the saying aptly summarizes the time I've understood about this country. There are, of course, outliers, those who do not exist at the average place in the clean/soiled spectrum, but it seems that because so many of this country have faced such difficulties, they've accepted the dirty car. There are those I've met who struggle to mitigate the state of their country's backseat, especially the youth I've encountered, but it seems to me that for every one Ukrainian who would take their empty cans with them, several would leave them in the cupholders. All they've known is a dirty car, and what's one more wrapped on the floor behind them.

Therein lays the greatest mental challenge I've encountered here. It is one I have long been unaware of and deeply affected by, but is, at last, apparent: it's hard for me to live in a country where so many things are accepted, so many problems taken at face value, as the normal course of life, while simultaneously I am encouraged, by my setting and my place within it, to meditate on my own mortality. I am led, by the daily commute which takes me past the cemeteries, the hospital, the bus station, and the eateries, by the full circle of life available to my view every time I wander the village avenues, by the whole of existence in a village that can be grasped from any one of the nearby hills, to remember how fickle is my existence.

The memory of my being stands before me, as the hollow buildings in the abandoned part of town. Their windows have been shattered, their floors have fallen through, their original purpose has long been forgotten. Their future is inevitable, no matter how hard we may ignorantly, productively, or frantically we rage against it. How can I reconcile my present to these testaments to my future? No matter how well these structures were built, how cherished they were in their use, they are all equalized by time. Grey, abandoned, and indistinguishable

What's the difference, Michelle, between a statue and the woman on the corner who sells crabapples and canned mushrooms, who waits for her pension to be doled out to her by a casual shopper? What the difference between that edifice and that woman in her wheelchair, placed near a garden until the orderly returns?

There is little to distinguish them. Both are adorned, by marble, or makeup, flowers, or flower print. Both are unmoving, with a melancholy etched in their eyes. The answer, then, is that, in time, the memorials will be remembered.

So I'm left with my existential musings, more gray thoughts for gray days. At least, now, after leaving, absent of them for a little while, I finally recognize their source. Perhaps knowing that will allow me greater control of them.

Happy New Year.

Pensively,

Sam.

P.S.: While rereading this letter, the morning after I signed my name to its conclusion, I noticed, upon a closer examination of my words and from a perspective more objective than when I wrote them, that you may receive the impression that I have wholly condemned the village life, the society of my home. Please, if this is what you're led to feel, allow me to rectify this impression, soften the impact of my description.

While I know I can be quite dramatic, particularly when I am allowed pen and paper and little distraction in the small hours of the night, I must insist that the great majority of my time here has been wonderful. I have tried to communicate this in previous letters, and feel I must reiterate the sentiment, given the tone and subject matter of this communication. Furthermore, though extremely unqualified to do so, I made note of an issue I have with the way some Ukrainians see their own country. This is far from the only impression I have received from my interactions with my community here, it is simply the most recently significant one. As well, just because I voice concern with a phenomena I see here does not mean I consider my own country to be blameless. In fact, my experiences in Ukraine have led me to reconsider several aspects of life at home, the foremost being questions I'd love to ask my own culture, perhaps the most alien I'd ever experience had I not been born into it:

Do we truly believe that because of our own self-imposed significance we can cheat what no one ever has? From the outside looking in, the American dream does not appear to be anything its purported to be. It isn't wealth. It's not prosperity, or comfort. Perhaps it was at one point; certainly these are still the dreams of those for whom the fundamental tenets of American progress and economic reward are still beyond them. I can't speak for those who can no longer dream, or for those whose dreams have been limited by life circumstances I am privileged to be unfamiliar with. As a whole, however, today the American dream seems to be more a societal ploy for immortality. If I can make myself powerful, successful, famous enough, I can keep myself alive, culturally. Whether through a biopic or a hologram, resurrection is within reach.

Our statues are digital, the hallowed halls are overcrowded.

Those people who deserve to be appreciated after their time are supplanted. They're appreciated for too short a time, in their own time.

Legacy is virtual, it lasts forever and is replaced instantly.

Is this what happens when a society collectively disassociates from death? Gone are the reminders of our own mortality, our cemeteries are outside of town, our feeds are tailored to what we desire to see.

Can we let anything die?

If you see it the way I do, this inquiry feels far more damning, and of a much greater import than a dirty car. Perhaps a trip to a village somewhere in Eastern Europe, while certain to trigger various existential crises, would refresh all our perspectives in a way we all need them to be.

8.

Dear Michelle,

I feel I'm not collecting stories anymore.

Wouldn't it be helpful if jet streams stopped for an outstretched thumb? Without a car, and at the mercy of a, diplomatically put, capricious system of public transport, I often feel trapped by this village. That the main road and rail throughways between the grand Ukrainian cities of Uzhhorod and L'viv pass astride my apartment is a chronic irony, an open window set high the walls of a cell: unattainable, yet persistently aspired to. Of little comfort, a mocking hope.

A few of my colleagues have hitchhiked, taken rides from strangers from village to town. While their stories are encouraging. I can't bring myself to do it.

If I had a car here, I probably wouldn't go anywhere. But I'd like the freedom to.

I'd like a ladder to that window, even if I'm complacent enough for these walls.

Incidentally, is there a way to express the sentiment that fences appear petty in an airplane window without it sounding like a bit of incorrigibly prepubescent philosophy? In theory, the thought sounded great, glancing at the massive cast-iron gates of a few of my neighbors a few days ago, bemusedly noting how little they would prevent, if anyone ever actually committed theft in a town this small, where in less than a few hours one could surely discover the culprit and politely ask for their property back, but in practice, it feels a trite observation. I don't know. I suppose everything looks serene from 30,000 feet.

This was the same morning I considered how much it would alter human perspective if our species were capable of being squashed out of existence in an unpredictable instant, akin to the slug whose remains I struggled to fully remove from in between my shoe treads when I arrived at the office.

I was moody, that is to say, in a mood.

Which, I think, stemmed from this feeling. That I'm no longer collecting stories.

I can't go back and read through them, and I hope I never have to, but I'm assured the collective tone of my letters to this point has been far from cheerful. Themes of longing, the archetype of the weary, forlorn traveler, the forced introspection tinged with regret, permeate. Thank you for giving these stories their time, despite the angst. Despite their impression. I cherish your compassionate responses and imply the regrets of your own which you withhold from your pen, for my sake. In between your crisp lines is the silent entreaty, the admonishment, the "What did you expect?" Yet, absent your heart, you encourage me, and through it all, I've adopted your excitement. Although the moments were difficult: instances of arrival, overstimulation, adjustment, or reflection, the stories saved me. Those excited and blissful narrations, while I marveled at the pure experience of living abroad and alone, saved me. Whatever the variable emotion, the snapshot reality, the image was subsumed by a collection, comprising a comfortingly grand image. Fleeting struggles were merely a part of a greater story, and I was living it.

The forest of life is good, the trees are only what is necessary.

When I was in the 7th, 8th, and 9th grades, the late years of what you call elementary school (what the more grounded among us call grade school) and my first of high school, I attended a boarding school. Maybe I've mentioned this offhandedly, or, more likely, we've discussed my time here at length, or, most likely, the effects of those years are so etched in my personality or characteristics you required no elucidation, I can't remember, yet I sense little need to expound on the idea. What matters is that I attended a private, Catholic boarding school for three years, and one of the myriad rules I was subjected to, were the limits placed on our interactions with family. We were away from home to be separated from the world; they intended us to become our own family. What we came from, though enduring, was a distraction. Our home was the school, and to foster this purportedly-crucial sense of presently-communal connectivity, we were allowed one phone call a week.

Initially, I could never think of anything to say. A week of a 15 year-old's time was too vast in scope to be recollected with any great detail, and I recall the pain in my mother's voice when, week after week, the conversation died a quarter of an hour after it began. This was not for lack of trying, but I simply could not condense a week into an hour; I could not hope to remember it all, so I remembered nothing.

Then, one night, on a visit to the *Tiendiata*, the name we gave our little student-run marketplace and prayed the Dean never inspected the books of, I found a little flip notebook to compliment my shift's portion of stolen Strawberry Shortcakes. The flimsy pad had a red cover, was maybe a hundred pages, and reminded me of the notepads TV detectives walked around with and flipped open for dramatic effect. S

In this pocket journal, I began documenting everything of note that happened to me. Within weeks, I found the allotted hour insufficient, and would stay on the phone long into night, regaling each of my siblings with the assortment of stories alluded to by their headnotes. Since none of my classmates ever utilized the full hour, and none of the staff had the heart to tell me to hang up on my parents, I discovered that with these stories, I could not only make my parents happy, feel connected with them in a profoundly new way, and share a lovely, rambling, weekly conversation, but on those phone call nights I could miss dinner, the night activity, and night prayers in their entirety, and, while my peers slept, scrounge the deserted kitchen for every donated donut and bulk fruit cocktail can my heart desired. My nocturnal feasts in that magically-echoing and hauntingly-empty building became my sanctuary. I would sit in that grand dining hall, at any seat I preferred, listen to the scratching of my fork reverberate with the clunking of the cast-iron heaters, rest my wooden-heeled feet on the chair across mine, and eat slowly, deliberately, and in peace. On such occasions, I snuck into the dormitory with a wide and satisfied smile. These nights were the only time that was my own, a refuge in a rigid schedule. And the only way I could carve out time for them was if I had saved enough to tell when the phone rang for me.

Thus I collected, burning through those little notebooks like the most detail-oriented detective the precinct had ever seen. My friends grew accustomed to my scribbling, and if I ever misplaced the worn pages, they were returned to me instantly. Soon, they were asking to borrow them for their own phone calls, and I began carrying one in each back pocket: one for ours, and one for my own.

Nowadays, I collect them on my phone.

If I am to die some horribly unforeseen death, like a slug underfoot a preoccupied commuter, and if the world ever achieves the technology portrayed in that "Be Right Back" Black Mirror episode, know the notes app in my phone contains more than enough datapoints to properly resurrect my consciousness. There is collected my every notable thought, every worthwhile moment, every quote I found impressionable, and every piece of art I hope to yet to be impressed by. And, of course, there are stories.

I started a new folder when I arrived at Peace Corps staging. Since my summer internship in D.C., this has been my tradition. A new stage for stories, a new place to collect them. New beginnings, new folders. I don't know if you remember me showing you the one named "My Summer with Louise", but it's replete with nearly every experience I felt would have earned a place on the weekly phone call. For my time in Ukraine, I tried being clever and titled my current periodical repository: "Tales from the Breadbasket", an overt nod to Ukraine's cognomen while a member state of the Soviet Union.

My last entry in this folder came over a month ago, a few weeks after I postmarked my last letter. The entry reads: "tiger in the parade", but I don't remember typing it, and haven't the slightest idea the story it's referring to.

I'm not collecting stories.

Phone calls would hardly see me past the soup course. I'd start, catch the familiarity, understand I've told this story, or one similar, stutter for a time, search my memory for something else to say, then grudgingly rejoin my peers and blow my spoon cold with a dejected air. What stories I'd relate would be curtailed by indifference, halved by monotony, or waived by similarity: Unfriendly neighbors when the kettle screamed too long, the strange, melancholic, and ever-present carnival rides like our town's own Chernobyl, an awkward English club when the one success I've had became mired as one of the kids asked me to show a Eurovision video. I did, and two minutes into the song a naked, underwater silhouette filled the screen, and myself and the librarian with horror.

Whatever the reason for the arid well, its stories are stifled.

I am stifled, perhaps, because I draw stories from my interactions with others, and here, I don't think we see each other as real people. The vast differences between myself and my community, and the expectations gleaned from these distinctions, have rendered us near caricatures in each other's eyes. The person with whom I interact with most, oft the only person I will talk to for days at a time, my counterpart, is a young woman, a mother, a daughter to a town elder, a native of this village, a Ukrainian citizen, with a job she's worked at for years, and a life well established before I ever entered it. A young American, a boy, adrift, apart from his home, a resident of a place of which she's never heard, a volunteer who has never held a full-time job, is explaining to her how to better do hers. Of course she is apt to discredit me! Of course I view perfect assimilation, perfect trust, impossible! We are playing chess with checker pieces, trying to know each other, knowing we never will, and that, likely, we have attempted all we can. What stories are there to be told between two who will always be strangers?

Perhaps it's deeper than that. Perhaps I can find no stories because there was only ever one.

More and more of late, I've felt constrained in my interactions, felt a limit to the depths of my relationships, felt a distinct and stalwart point of connection and that beyond which is inaccessible. As I've come to know the community, as they've come to know me, the clearer my role becomes and the more I understand that what binds me is my home.

I am bound by America.

I am their access to the American Dream, their sole chance at recovering what small portion of that prosperity is due them, made available to them through the privileged nation's limited alms. I read a schoolbook describing the beauty of my country, I read in Ukrainian that the United States is the most developed nation in the world, and I finally understand the breadth of my fortune, why I was invited, what is expected of me, and, how utterly ignorant I am of the means to attain it for them. Coupled by the consuming desiring to bestow on my community everything they wish from me, all that is available to me because of my passport that would make their lives better, I am left paralyzed, stalemated by the ill-begotten task.

The few occasions I have attempted to cross that barrier, to delve further into a cooperation with my coworkers, my neighbors, my community, I sense a sickening parallel to that of the horror a used car salesman if he were ever forced to listen to the recordings of his sleazy dealings. I stand in front of a collection of individuals whose years all outnumber my own, whose wisdom is true and specific and necessary and not accorded them by a guaranteed education, and while I wait for my words to be dictated in Ukrainian, the eagerness of all attendees apparent without translation, their eyes screaming their reliance, their desperation for this boy to bring them out of poverty, their first and perhaps only lifeline to a life outside their own, their hope unfounded, I feel the staggering weight of my empty words, and I want to run to my room, lock the door, and save us all the charade. Despite my instructions, I know the solution to their struggles is not in time management. I know none of them will ever write a business plan, and I know that a calendar will go unused after a week. I am standing in the spotlight and wishing I were invisible; the eyes of the room are on me, and I have nothing to give them but the false enthusiasm of a man with nothing to sell but must do it anyway.

I feel as empty there, here, as I ever have. I wish I were invisible. I may as well be invisible. I am at the nexus of an impossibly comprehensive, collaborative effort to render from life human being, but rather than live up to this awareness, I feel oppressed by it.

Where's the story in that?

Arthur Miller has already told it.

Sullen, with an addendum of what I have collected of late, too brief to be stories and too raw to be poems, included before I forget why I thought to preserve them,

Sam

Fluid Brutalism.

or:

Collected Fragments of Thought from a Young Mind in a
Strange Place, Saved in the Notes App

1.

He was carried out of his room. He watched movies from his
window, but he needed to be outside. Along the creaking floors of
bubbling tile, past rooms with tea sets from the local bazaar painted
to look like they were from faraway lands, drying apples and old
tomatoes, pill bottles and dusty photos, unused couches and large
rugs adorning the rest, he moved.

She was in the kitchen, watching her weekly programs. He told
her he was leaving to borrow a book from a friend. It was the first
thing that came to mind, and he knew the word for book.

On the outside, he had gone to get a cup of coffee before a
phone call. With his parents, their conversation was sure to be both
full of love and too long. What was his past was remote, distant,
and meant to be behind. He was a good son. But he was here and
they were there.

Was it selfish to hold that against them?

He strode to the nearest plaza. Drink in hand, he sat beside
Shevchenko.

At this crossroads he shared a bench with five others. Their
lives had intersected and they lived while he waited.

He tried to read. The words could not hold him. They were
not the story he came for.

Teenagers passed. Teenagers sat and talked. Each was
remarkably similar, down to the distinct aura of artificial

conformity that thrives in the young and unsure. A young girl shared a long hug with a friend, and then a short one with an acquaintance.

Couples walked oblivious, the world unnoticed.

An old man, face like Shevchenko, walked by in a pressed, grey suit. His gaze did not break. His destination was his only concern.

As life progresses, so too, its worries.

The setting sun blanketed all in twilight. In the dusk he forwent all pretense of reading and focused on a group of birds on the horizon, on the life surrounding this intersection, and on the absence of a tangible thought. His setting narrowed as his mind emptied. Something about the color in the sky, the shape of a bush, the face of a passerby, struct him. The mysteries, lives, he would never understand enveloped his gaze. The feeling was at once strange, and familiar. He was in tune with something he could not hold, yet it grabbed him all the same.

Transfixed, he smiled.

She was asleep when he returned, her head resting against the wall with the loud wallpaper as commercials fought silently against the oncoming night. The talk of the radio was softer.

He wanted to be alone.

2.

Journey's midnight train going anywhere could not compare to the one which cuts through central Ukraine.

This train is covered in the soot of its own coal fires, which feed excessive heat into the old and empty cabins. My pilling sweater goes nicely with the scarred wooden window frames nicely. Dark grey, the dark grey of a cloudy day in a sad place, hangs over the passing country, and is seen through plastic windows tinted with grime and framed by splintered wood.

We slowly pass a stone tower, red and white stone, the last testament to a factory whose only product now is the crumbling cement and metal of its build. If there was a sun, there would be a shadow, and the village would lay in it.

There is one flame in one window. It is the only flame on this Wednesday evening. I wonder when its occupants knew when they were never going to leave this place before we turn a corner, and I wonder who is better for it.

3.

The man across the yard is a mover in brutalism

The only other light on

We watch each other sometimes

Because we know we will never meet

He smokes his cigarette

His pulsing light

before closing his window and returning
to the violent white kitchen TV

while my data is drained by soundless YouTube

4.

In the late afternoon of a rainy day,

When the man across the street was preparing his nightly position as the smoker in the window,

On a lonely lake where two swans rested

Their white coats against the grey apartments and the brown, dead shore grass

Where in the stillness I heard a cough

From the distant brutal building

And since I could not see from whom it came or from which balcony

It seemed to me that the structure itself has made the noise,

I met an old man, the only other figure in the somberly peaceful setting

A bird watching, Russian dentist.

I came towards him,

Carrying many worries,

Chief among them whether I would slip in the muddy path and

Whether he would ask me for money.

I was unfair to both of us.

I pulled my hat down, the hat I used to hide my long hair,

And he asked me in Russian if I saw the swans.

"Of course I do," I said, in Ukrainian, "they're beautiful."

The man in the bright red jacket then questioned me,

"Where are you from?"

Maybe it was my accent, or maybe it is what strangers ask to learn more about each other.

"Poland", I lied.

"Poland! Wow!" He said ringing across the pit of a lake.

"I am Russian," said the man with the dirty boots.

"Do you have a family?", he clasped his hands.

"Yes", I replied.

"What's important is family," he said, "then love and health."

I agreed, and he wished these things for me. He said he was 70, he felt 20, and that he could not imagine watching TV on a night like this.

Then he blasted on his bird caller and offered a hand.
"My Russian isn't great."

He turned to leave,

and I remembered my wet feet,

My shopping list,

My imbalance,

My disappointment with the wet trash on the ground,

My anxiety for the bad news which had driven me from the apartment.

I was the first to want to move on, but he was the first to do so,

And the old man with the youthful soul,

The nature lover and family practitioner,

Left me to recollect my worries and start on again.

5.

There's a simple beauty in the Ukrainian countryside

Grass grows over

abandoned homesteads

And forests flourish.

Here a young boy sprinkles feed

To chickens

On a Sunday morning

And my train goes East.

6.

Grey again,

gray in everything, the world in a gray filter

Smoke passes over tin roofs with mold and age

A man in Black, a black hat and black jacket and white hair sneaking out of it sits on a bar of purposeless concrete

Next to mud and a pool of water in the gravel road

And he stares into his hands

A bag with a logo of a car he's never seen carries enough food for the day and vodka in a plastic bottle

An empty grain tower towers above him

Behind the cluttered balconies boxes of light flickered off as their inhabitants allowed the sheer grey facade to once more stand imposing in its darkness

On the concrete log

Waiting for something

Watching something in the muddy water below.

7.

It seems as though the bleak and imposing facades are undone by the light,

accentuate the individual brightness and achieve the opposite of their desired effect

9.

"The most transparent something was, the more mysterious it seemed. The universe itself was transparent as long as you were sufficiently sharp-eyed, you could see as far as you liked. But the farther you looked, the more mysterious it became."

Liu Cixin

Dear Michelle,

Are you better off for having known me?

I ask this, hoping my directness might express the sincerity with which I pose the question.

It's a question, as you well know, I dwell upon often, directed at you, personally, or at my sliver of encountered humanity, as a whole. It's a question I contemplate between the top and fitted sheets, one which demands an answer in the loneliest moments in my life, an impossibly query I ask only when it is impossible for anyone to answer.

You know this.

You know, as a people person yourself, how paralyzing, encompassing, obsessing, this question can be. One question which captures my immature morality. Immature, because I am so desperate for an answer eternally unforthcoming.

If I can only better the lives of everyone I touch, I will have lived well.

This question plagues me now, Michelle, like never before, because I feel like I am somewhere outside of where I might have been meant to be. Had I remained where I was, I ought not to have focused on my impact quite as much, but being in such a foreign and unfamiliar place as this, where I know, unequivocally, that everyone I encounter is encountered by me solely because I made the conscious decision, the long journey, the unfounded promise, to come here, I find myself asking it often. Are you better off for having known me, little village for whom I would always have been the perfect strange had I never imposed myself upon it?

When I arrived, I committed to my colleagues, however inadvertently, at the city council, progress, change, betterment. I was removed from my position a few days ago. After months of stalled progress, the mayor requested I be taken immediately from his purview. Are my colleagues better off for having known me?

If I had taken a less self-directed path, I might not have struggled with the implications of my decisions as heavily. Now, though, aware I came halfway across the world to disappoint an entire community, lives who would never have otherwise been affected by my unfounded self, the negative implications of our interactions are all the stronger. I came to them, and time and time again in this country I have let them down. Is this at all fair to those who never wished to be affected by me in the first place? How dare I impose my personal conflict upon them, how dare I arrive unsure, fractured, timid, how dare I let my internal struggles effect the work upon which they hung so much hope! Work which was the sole means by which they might judge my impact in their lives! How can I reconcile what has happened with who I wish to be, knowing that, entirely of my own doing, I came, I saw, and I was soundly self-defeated, that all which remains in the village zeitgeist of their first American are memories of his absences, his hesitation to fully commit, his unspoken reservations, his unsevered ties to what he left behind. These conflicts were not for them, they were internal, but they were felt by all, all the same.

How should they know me otherwise, save the impressions I offered?

Please do not think me self-indulgent, as if my impact on their lives was so profound that it must be judged. Most people go unnoticed by most, with time. But, by nature of my presence, I was different. I was not some incidental encounter, I was applied for and planned for, thus my impact was noted, and felt. My community was living its collective lives perfectly well without me, and, whatever their answer to my prologuing question, they continue to do so now that I have left them.

I express these sentiments in no way propounding my own significance. I have heard Carl Sagan's *Blue Dot*; I know how trivial I am.

But that doesn't stop me from feeling immense, like Atlas bowed by the weight of the world, so the great significance of the part I played in the recent life of this village is burdened by the enormity of this question. Is Perechyn, is my counterpart, my office, my host mother, father,, sister, is the English club, is the mayor, is the place, so utterly microcosmic, better, for having known me?

I was no passing fancy.

Rather, while I dwell on the entirety, hiding in my apartment, at the behest of Peace Corps' headquarters, from the border guards who have been informed my work visa was retracted, I am convinced that, for the brief time we shared, our lives are forever changed, whether by the good, or by the deeply unresolved.[13]

I will tell you the rest of the story when I know how it ends. I doubt I will be able to mail this until then.

Apprehensively,

Sam

---

[13] It's possible that my impact feels so singularly inflated because in this one, unflinching case, my impact was so apparently negative and thus I must have been more to these people than I may have been otherwise. Don't we all recall the disappointments more clearly than the triumphs?

An Intermission.

"The proper function of man is to live, not to exist. I shall not waste my days in trying to prolong them. I shall use my time."

Jack London

Dear Michelle,

You asked me to provide you with a little more context for my last and short and emotional letter.

I've always heard that art, via the senses by which it is perceived, fills the soul. Certainly, when music renders goosebumps, when a painting demands attention, when a film becomes an experience, this sentiment is profoundly ratified. But, what if art, rather than fills us, demonstrates our fullness. Forces us to see the fullness of who we already are. What if, by bringing us to forgotten memories, dormant until that exact sequence of crescendoing musical notes, art is not what is behind the door, but the key to the door itself, beyond which waits, locked away in deference to subsequent experience. What if art does not offer anything, but, rather, draws something forth. What if it elicits. What if it evokes. What if it exists to reveal our selves to ourselves. What if, instead of needing to be filled, we are, in experience of beauty, simply made aware of how full and beautiful our lives already are.

I believe this is a much more pressing lens with which to judge the necessity of art in our lives.

Artists fashion the keys to our dead selves; great artists are those whose keys fit many locks.

Take images, for example. Photos, which, like art, like keys, may not mean anything but for the few meant to understand them, meant to be affected by them, meant to be opened by them.

Recently, in my own life, pictures have become ever more precious. I know, with the intensity of what my present life is, I am incapable of experiencing in totality these "epochal" memories. I understand I will need them drawn out of me, unlocked when I can better hope to hold, appreciate, experience, their fullness.

I've tried writing you the story of my removal from the village more times than I'd care to count. I've sat, a cooling cup of coffee and a soft playlist in my ears, waiting for the memory. I've started with a sentence: "I was ambushed yesterday," I've started with themes of the growing resentment which led to my firing, the passive disappointment, a monitoring catalyst, then active frustration concluding with coordinated sabotage, I've started from the end, when I was scolded on my way out of the mayor's office that my idea for a training on time management was like an alcoholic trying to teach people how not to drink vodka, I've started with a title: Tell Me Their Names.

There is nothing, however, for me to write. An inexhaustibility is happening, and thus I cannot hold onto anything. Each day is replaced by the essentialness of the next, and concentration is fixed forcibly on the present. What is remembered is stored. So I take pictures, and I wait for them to become the keys I will need on empty days like today.

On a quiet afternoon in my new apartment, I sat down with a few of these photos. These are their memories.

* * *

I took a picture on a train. Outside, the frozen countryside was blanketed by the bottomless world of darkness. The Soviet-era cars swayed heavily as they sliced through the night. I was riding the overnight from a small village in the neighboring oblast to my new service city. The journey had started well, I boarded to find two women and their children, who immediately took to the strange-looking stranger and asked me questions at an accessible language level, occupying the other beds in our small coupe. After I had won over the kinds, their parents loosened their stern expressions and we stumbled through a cooperative conversation about what the real America was like. They disagreed with many of the experiences I related of my home, having seen otherwise in film or YouTube. When we were interrupted by an errant toy plane, or a demand to judge a marker drawing, I was grateful. Eventually, our dialogue gave way to a heated debate between the two women over who was more correct about their opinions about my country which conflicted with their own, and I took to making my own drawings and my own erratic tossing of the toy planes. Later, I was invited to join them for home-brought sandwiches and vodka, an apparent staple of inter-Ukraine travel. We were all smiles, and soon past discord was forgotten for fast-paced rounds of the card game "Loser". When I climbed to my top bunk and laid my head on a knotted pillow, I felt more at home than I ever had in a four-capacity foreign train car. I was relieved. Until I awoke to the stifling heat of the coal-burning furnaces, assaulted by the apparition of an absolutely putrid aroma. After a quick check to confirm my worst fears had not been realized (i.e., I was not the source of the stench), I investigated. In the low light of the safety guidelights spilling through the cracks of the heavy coupe door, I spotted the straps of a used diaper peeking out from the bed below me. Someone had placed it in the bread bag which had carried the sandwiches used to make what it now held, but whatever attempt had been made to seal the new contents had proved futile. With the taste of bile in my mouth, I scrambled off my bed and into the hallway. There, after a precious couple breaths of largely-untainted air, I took a picture: The long, rocking hallway that runs alongside the rooms. The light at the ended, clouded by a dusty cover which had not been cleaned in a decade, flickering for effect. The aisle is carpeted by a long, red runner which bore the remains of a pattern on its battered surface. The sealed windows are latched, their pale curtains sway. Underneath is a wooden handlebar which runs alongside the car. A sole outlet sits on the middle of the photo, beside a chair that folds out of the wall, set aside for the fortunate passenger who finds the socket empty. I spend most of my night here, listening to the click of the train's wheels, the screech of its brakes. Soon, I am asleep.

I took a picture in a school bathroom, in a village a few hours on a mashrutka from my new home. I had travelled there to help with an English summer camp, and to spend time with fellow volunteers. Our nights were filled with drinks and laughter and the comforts of the home we found in each other, reading screenplays inspired by the listless middle moments of our service, freezing showers, hot cowboy coffee, and late hours of the kind of rambling sleepover conversation I described in a previous letter. Our days were filled with laughing children, cafeteria lunches, and chance attempts at learning activities while the bored summer faculty, annoyed by their school system's camp requirement but grateful to delegate complete control to the inexplicably enthusiastic volunteers, sat beneath a nearby oak and drank homemade wine. Most of our spontaneous curriculum centered around us shepherding the class through the center of town and then chasing each other throughout the riverside nature area under a loose set of game rules. The experience was welcome and wholesome, and the week went by without significant event until, in preparation for another day in the park, I sprayed myself in the eye with sunscreen in a village school bathroom whose sinks all lacked running water. What was a lovely morning became one of the more uncomfortable in my life. Once my sight had adjusted, my yelping subsided, and I could blink through the film of water, I recognized the comedic absurdity of the situation. I took a picture: My eyes are bloodshot, and my eyelids betray my tears. I am wearing a collection of thrifted clothes, and I can hardly see where I am pointing the camera. I hear a student coming to use the bathroom, so I click the shutter quickly before ducking into a stall to avoid being seen in this state. I am smiling.

I took a picture of myself, breathing heavily, with a guitar strung across my back. After the camp, where, desperate for a hobby and currently out of work, I had purchased a cheap acoustic guitar from my host, I returned to my village one last time before I was to be relocated. I was embarrassed to be back and did my best to avoid notice. When I recognized a former coworker boarding two stops before my own, I rushed from my seat to avoid being seen. After a few moments to collect myself, I began walking home, instead, and realized I had left the instrument behind. for the individual wishing to remain anonymous, an all-out sprint down the road after a bus he had only just exited was certainly inopportune. I caught up to the vehicle at the central station and shared an uncomfortably-pointed eye contact with my colleague while I collected my belongings. When I stepped off again, drenched in sweat and immortalized in her mind as the frantic, helpless, and quite possibly, foolish, American, I decided to immortalize the moment for myself as well, a supposed turning point. Not for my characteristics, but for my assessment of them. I took a picture: It was my Inside Llewyn Davis moment. The frazzled outsider, learning to accept himself. Inside Sam Luebbers, if you will. In the background of the selfie was the last image of the village I ever took. There is a bread stand in the corner, and the bench outside the bus station was vacant and crooked.

I took a picture from months earlier and spliced it with a picture of Spencer from the Disney Channel show iCarly. This was at another summer camp, further from my new home at a sleepaway event center tucked into the easternmost slopes of the Ukrainian Carpathians. It was here, while helping to conduct events, leading a team of campers, and enjoying the experience of hands-on, organized, and comprehensive youth development, where I embraced my persona, if only for the week. In a space for all the participants, camper and counselor alike, to step outside their lives, meet new people, and learn from one another, the atmosphere was one of acceptance and camaraderie, which led us all towards truer versions of ourselves. I was the counselor-clown, photobombing a photo-sessions, conducting a daily chorus of Queen's Bohemian Rhapsody, which I was incredibly surprised and proud to find these young Ukrainians knew by heart, scavenging extra perogies with the other slow eaters, performing different characters for the kids who enjoyed the antics, performing the "Riddles in the Dark" section of the Hobbit as Gollum and doing the voice for kids whose blank expressions explained too late that they had only ever seen the dubbed version and that they hadn't the slightest idea of what Andy Serkins actually sounded like, accidentally leaping into a nest of stinging nettle to motivate some of the campers less inclined to summit the mountain that was our day's activity. I was the friend to all, playing chess with the reserved, discussing classes with the ambitious, running around with the wild, and laughing with them all. We all were everyone we'd ever been, in our own way, and for someone whose reality was presently in flux, caught in between forces over which he had no control, the temporary removal was intoxicatingly refreshing. One night, while sitting around a campfire in traditional last day of summer camp fashion, a few of my team claimed to have discovered my doppelgänger. When I told them to get off their phones and marvel at the sublime clarity of the stars, they showed me a picture of Spencer, and after discussing each other's look-alikes, we talked about the wage gap, micro-aggressions, and stereotypes. Vastly different from the topics I knew to cover at their age. Before we went to bed, I cropped the two pictures together and sent them to my team's GroupMe. I also took a picture of the stars: but these never turn out. I won't describe the blurred beings, the interstellar spectacles rendered streaks of grey by my shaky grip and my phone's prolonged exposure setting. However, I know nothing could ever capture the intensity of the universe seen from deep within the Ukrainian countryside. Its light defies art, and in them are the keys to any self that has ever existed, or will exist.

I took a picture of the hostel I first stayed in after being relocated to my new city, Uzhhorod. I was waiting for my housing situation to be arranged and, in the meantime, was receiving a weekly hotel allowance. When I initially arrived, I pocketed most of this per diem and stayed in the cheapest room I could find. However, on my third night, when I woke up at 4:00 am to a heavenly light, only to discover it was the phone flashlight of a very drunk Russian-speaking teenager who was aggressively claiming I was in his bed, I decided right away to look for more private accommodations. Somehow, however, in the moment, I ended up apologizing, though I had been in the same bunk for days, and re-made it for him before climbing to the top and spending the rest of my waking night in a very confused and anxious state. I took a picture: His clothes were strewn over the floor, and the overhead light was on. One leg spilled out from underneath my bed, and a roommate and I shared an exasperated look. At the bottom of the image are my headphones and my free Delta sleep mask, then both staples of any trip I took within my service country's borders. I had encountered enough intoxicated fellow travelers to know how to best deal with them.

I took a picture of a friend and a cobblestoned alleyway. If before was an Inside Llewyn Davis moment, this could be most closely likened to a Midnight in Paris moment; the scenery was equally stunning, the streets, streetlamps, and facades equally reminiscent of a time long since passed, and myself equally romantic about the prospects of living in an unrecoverable moment, everything was the same, up to the tolling of the church bells at midnight, but absent the love interest. A new friend, a young Ukrainian woman whom I had met the local university's previously-established English club and who worked as a translator for an American oil company, and I roamed the streets of her home. She pointed out the historical structures, her favorite restaurants, and general charm of the quaint, old city. I took a picture at the bottom of a side street: The paving was cobblestone, a nightmare for the worn shocks of the vehicles which passed us, but a dream for me. The city's lights were soft, and I imagined the avenue would look most itself under the cover of a soft, untouched snow. Ahead was the steeple of a domed church built centuries before its attendants spoke Ukrainian, and alongside us was a strip of pubs, whose latticed windows spilled a welcoming warmth into the brisk summer evening.

I took a picture of a painting and a painter, engaged in a local tradition of painting the cherry trees during the annual Cherry Blossom Festival. The city was alive, its trees and streets vibrant, the sidewalks lined with vendors of artisan goods and watched over by blooms of luminescent pink. The trees had been gifted to the city by some Japanese delegates generations ago and were an essential part of present-day Uzhhorod. I took a picture: He was old and bowed, not a touch of pretention about his paint-smeared smock, worn brushes, and intent expression. He was as true a storied artist as I am ever to find. He was unaffected by my lingering amazement of his profoundly-simple, practiced talent, and only asked I tag him in the picture if I ever posted it to Facebook.

I took a picture of a bus window. In Ukraine, I discovered a more topical fear of the draft than the one we had learned about during the 1960's. Many of the older generation here hold onto a plethora of superstitions, and devoutly adhere to their axioms. I think I told you about the time I was nearly scared to death when my host grandmother slammed the bathroom door open to yell at me to stop whistling indoors? Well, another fear which many elderly Ukrainians impose upon their worlds is the fear of any sort of draft. If there is a window open in the kitchen, they will close every other window in the house. Someone told me that it's believed the draft will bring a chill, which will lead to a cold, but I find it difficult to believe there is not also some supernatural bent to the practice, of the kind most traditions in this country can trace their origins to. This practice is dramatically applied to the younger generation's penchant for avoiding heat stroke on public transportation, i.e., opening the windows on busses and trains. Every time the un-air-conditioned mass reaches a boiling point, a brave millennial representative will open a single window, as nonchalantly as the tepid air allows. After, the tension will be palpable, as the rest wait for the response of any elder women in accompaniment. If they are unperturbed, the humidity will increase one last time as the whole of the throng breathes a muggy sigh of relief, but it is a turning point, and soon all the windows are unlatched and fresh, cool air whips through the grateful bus. More often than not, however, the trial window is resoundingly slammed shut, and the poor volunteer roundly reprimanded for his brazen act. I took a picture: An annoyed teen smirked at me while a tiny woman wrapped in a shawl and unsettlingly unaffected by the heat wagged a finger to emphasize that putting others in danger was nothing to smile about. The bus is yellow, and its handlebars are hot to the touch.

I took a picture of a picture. It was the moment in the movie Sandlot when the Beast jumps to swallow the catapulted ball whole. I was sitting in the back of the classroom, relishing the reactions of my new English club. I took a picture: The students were on their feet, jeering, screaming, laughing, all in broken English. This was my new home, and I was happy for it.

I took a picture of a tiny closet. This was the city's most-well-known print shop, tucked into a residential home on the corner of the main square. I took a picture: my coworker could hardly stand straight while she waited to collect the color certificates of achievement we were to give the attendants of our Disability Awareness training.

I took a picture of the ground outside the door to my apartment, and a curled piece of charred paper. Having never used a gas oven before, especially one without a pilot light, it's a miracle I haven't blown myself up yet. My apartment is on the third floor of a quintessentially Soviet apartment building, boasts a balcony on either side, an empty TV stand, a couch that serves as my bed, a breakfast nook, a toilet in a green-tiled room separate from the shower and sink, a washer, several iconographic depictions of Jesus, his mother, and his disciples, and a modest kitchen, littered with the belongings of the former tenant: an old woman and the mother of my new landlady. I use her mugs every morning, and her cast-iron pan coated with infinite meals every night. This is my new spot, my favorite place in the world, and every morning I wake up excited for the chance to drink coffee and watch my neighbors in the apartment courtyard from my rear-facing balcony or the bustle of the city from my front-facing one. My second evening in the apartment, hoping to make a homemade pizza, I nearly sent it all to hell. I turned on the gas and shoved a small handheld light down into the depths of the hissing, cavernous metal box. Once I smelled natural gas but did not see a flame issuing from my hand, I quickly withdrew it. A cursory Google search led me to realize I needed something thinner than my arm to reach the burners, so I grabbed the closest piece of paper I could find. Without letting the gas dissipate, I opened the oven's valve once more, shoved the rolled, burning paper within, and watched as, with a nearly-eyebrow-searing whoosh the burners ignited. Falling back, I hit my head against the table, and then spotted the flames licking hungrily down the paper towards my hand. In sort-of a panic, I flung the makeshift torch away, through the open window, and watched as it momentarily fluttered in the wind before plummeting to the ground. Relieved, I lean against the leg of the table, breathing heavily, until a quiet misgiving roared into a demand that I go inspect the scrap of paper that had survived the inferno. Sure enough, laying at the entrance to my building is a half-charred scrap of paper bearing my full name, date of birth, and social security number. I had taken the paper from the nearest available folder: a copy of the security check I had completed before acceptance into the Peace Corps. I took a picture: Behind the camera, I am smiling at this simple image that perfectly captures my experience to this point. I am a little burnt, a little thrown out, but I am still myself, and I will find the ground.

*   *   *

As I mentioned, I've tried writing more about my removal from my first site, my hurried relocation from my village. While I cannot say I enjoyed every moment, that place was my home for a precious time, and despite the many pictures which give access to myriad memories of those times, out of respect for those involved and for my unresolved feelings, I will refrain. What I can say, is that I will my friends. The life I'd established. Years from now, perhaps I'll write a story about it. For now, there is nothing else you need to know to follow my story than that I was removed by my mayor from what was supposed to be the position where I worked for the entirety of my two years. I am now in the beautiful city of Uzhhorod, with the piece of a new life to put together. I remain optimistic; determined to make the most of my time here.

Writing, rather than helping me remember, allows these moments the time they deserve. When I was living then, I was among so many others. Here, as I pen this, my mind is here. I think time flies because memory is imperfect. If we could hold onto everything entirely, life would feel very long, indeed.

Perhaps, a little too long. Each day I live, I lose a little more of who I was before. One day, I will think it better to stop losing than to gain. For someone who actively and often considers how best to extend his life, the thought is incomprehensible. Yet, if this weren't true, how else do so many relinquish their lives with such peaceful acceptance?

There is so much of my past I don't want to forget.

"Up till a minute ago it felt so real, but now it seems imaginary. Just a few steps is all it takes for everything associated with it to lose all sense of reality. And me – the person who was there until a moment ago – now I seem imaginary too." – Marukami, *Kafka on the Shore*.

Newly,

Sam

10.

"All the gods, all the heavens, all the hells, are within you"

Joseph Campbell

Dear Michelle,

Given the length of time that's transpired since my intermission note, I've summarized much of what has happened into these few pages. Please forgive me if these memoirs don't follow chronologically; tonight they've been arranged by spirit.

I typed a note to myself when I decided on the topic for my last letter. "Be sure to write about the other volunteers, how we affect each other," it reads. I think then, while I recounted a few of those sporadic stories, I understood something innate about recollection: where do we get more of our personal narrative than from our interactions with others?

So many of these stories are good. Moments so precious they are gifts to memory:

When I was removed from my village, I was saved by friendship. When I was defeated, the outward expression of the long-waged internal struggle I undertook when I first arrived at my site, I thought a lot about the volunteers who had chosen to end their involvement early. Where once I may have judged their reasoning, I found myself envious of their conviction. Though I had been quite literally ousted from my place of service, I knew I could never bring myself to leave. The assertiveness such an email would take had all been spent, years before, on a 4am message to my ROTC Colonel stating my intention to withdraw from the program days before we were to be flown to summer field training, and four years in the Air Force. I don't think I ever told you how spontaneous the decision truly was, or, although I initiated the conversation, how I could not bring myself to open my inbox in the days which followed because of the overwhelming apprehension I had for the response my sudden and decisive sentiment had elicited from my cadre. Thus, I bore the passing days in Ukraine, and, when I looked for renewal, I found it in connection, in the renewal of the bonds I shared with my peers.

I left a place I was dissatisfied with for a place I had never been, as our modern lives demand. Bearing the quintessential impetus for travel, after sixteen hours on a train, I completed the image of the perfect tourist. I climbed out of the car into a magnificent, iron station, the shade of the vaulted ceilings ensuring I could read the definitive hands of the enormous clock. Gathering my belongings, with a strap loose on my backpack and the zipper of my luggage bulging, I wandered outside. My eyes were unadjusted to the sudden glare of a midday sun, they were red with exhaustion and the heat of close quarters, and I stumbled my way downtown, putting the wheels of my rolling suitcase under some duress as they clattered over the cobblestone sidewalk. My friends, volunteers from several American cities I have yet to visit, waited for me at a café in downtown Kyiv. As I walked the streets, eyes glued to my digital map to save me from the unfamiliar corridors of the city, I grew accustomed to my insignificance, the foreign tags and foreign brands and foreign countenance drawing few looks from the pedestrians I encountered. I was comforted by this feeling, until, hoping to cut across a square which would lead me more quickly to my destination and was currently host to the starting line of the Kyiv Marathon. Thus my anonymity was immediately supplanted by a searing conspicuousness, as the strange backpacker wandered through a crowd of eager competitors, their bright athletic attire in sharp contrast to the dark, comfortable outfit I always wore when travelling overnight. The absurdity I experienced in the eyes of all who saw me went on to define the remainder of this wonderful trip, yet, once I was with the people who knew me, friends for whom the unfamiliar had become our norm, strangeness was replaced with comfort. It is so much easier to never know a stranger when it is not imperative, and, in the company of friends, the security of companionship accompanied us wherever we went. When we snuck into the hotel pool after it had closed, or wandered into an empty underground art gallery, or attended an event at the Canadian embassy in underwear which rank of chlorine but had gratefully dried before we were surrounded by international dignitaries, or played the Guinness game in a pub where for most of the other patrons it was a place where everyone knew your name, we could focus on being ourselves. The consuming sense of self-awareness we bore as strangers in a strange land was forgotten for the presence of just one familiar soul beside us. There was even solace to be found in the violent expulsion of several pints of Guinness the next morning; though I knew all 20 residents heard and mocked me, I knew one of them was my friend, and that made all the difference.

As well, there were times akin to these. When we volunteers were all brought together for our mid-service training, the phenomena of the adult sleepover I've previously described found us once again. Three grown men who spent the last five months in varying degrees of isolation in a room with each other equals three insomniacs who will have quite the conversation to look back on when they return to their far reaches of the country. The repeated experience left me to wonder why road trips and AA meetings are some of the very limited options adults have to be forced into interrogating conversations which have the space and time to grow into something more. There is clearly a need for more opportunities like these, in a world built on superficial interactions which leave us desperate for more. Perhaps, when I return to the states, I'll find a way to get you and everyone else I left behind in a car for a few days, that I might discover the full extent of the ineffable connections I was deprived of throughout my time here.

On America's Independence Day, a few of the aforementioned volunteers, and others, spent the night playing board games in an abandoned classroom of a conference center. Hereafter, we referred to the experience as "the 4th on the 4th", referring to the floor we had gathered on, and looked back on it fondly.

When a friend came to visit me in my new city, I had the courage to explore places I had long wanted to visit, and we soon found ourselves in an abandoned hotel participating in our first true Eastern European rave, which ended with us scooting down the uneven streets of downtown Uzhhorod on Razors we borrowed from his Airbnb at 4 am. The next morning (afternoon, as the clocks read), we greedily drank coffee and cocktails in a castle moat, under the watch of rampart walls, stone which has stood and will stand for centuries after we, and our hangovers, will pass.

In the town of a friend we played hacky sack in the ruins of an ancient fortress, the building's floors replaced by time with bright green grass, the roof with a clear blue sky. When an afternoon storm overtook the lush hills, the vision was indistinguishable from the Irish highlands, and we took it in in silence. Later, we, with the rest of the expat cohort who had made a home there, were asked to march in the parade that marked the end of a week-long festival celebrating the town, and with a face painted like a tiger I proudly smiled at the onlookers who lined the streets and cheered.

A group of us spent Christmas dinner with the gas company, when a carbon monoxide detector furnished by the Peace Corps sounded its alarm and the meal was abandoned for mulled wine while a steady stream of utility employees entered and exited the kitchen, each sharing a drink and a story with their enthralled foreign hosts.

One night, again in Kyiv, I shared a long conversation with an internationally-acclaimed and slightly racist author and his conspiracy-theorist bible-thumping friend while I waited for my phone to charge in the hostel common area.

I attended my first European soccer game, one of the few experiences I had actually intended when I selected Ukraine as my country of service. Any event so anticipated is bound to be a little underwhelming, but the brief interactions with the Ultras, a truly apocalyptic stadium bathroom experience, and a win, supplemented by a trip to a nearby planetarium whose last show was unattended, save for us, supplemented the night enough to ensure it would be memorable.

The true and easy friendship is hard to find, but any memory, made in the company of those with whom you can only be yourself, is surely precious.

However, not all stories are good. Some are not a gift, but a burden upon recollection:

While throwing up in the hostel bathroom was humorous, the effect it had on the hostel owner was anything but. As we checked out later that morning, I could sense our antics of the night before had undone our previous work of walking back the stereotypes he fostered for Americans. Where first we had stunned him with our grasp of his country, culture, and language, and had spent a lovely afternoon sharing the lunch his wife had packed for him while listening intently to the stories of his life and his family, upon our goodbye, his eyes glared. We were reduced, and returned to being just another group of privileged foreigners with no real care or regard for his home.

Somewhere along the timeline of our service a culture war erupted between the volunteers themselves. Cliques were formed and destroyed, angry messages were sent privately and discussed publicly, and the universal bonds we had arrived with were all but shattered. Unlike other circumstances involving the clash of ideologies, there were, truly, fine people on both sides of the argument, and most of us were deeply, individually saddened by the conflict as we watched from the sidelines of our isolated sites.

I met an expat who was the archetype of someone bound by their past, the embodiment of the prisoner tarot card. She was away from home to find herself, only to discover there are things which one cannot flee. Addiction does not abate upon escape. Her circumstance amplified my inner voice, its pleadings long ignored. There was nothing you did to make me leave, Michelle, and nothing you could have done to make me stay. I was running, not from something, but to the allure that, were my situation different, I may be, as well. She had a similar effect on us all.

Here, the contrasting effect of these memories holds me in place at my desk.

Later, I wonder:

'On the Good and the Bad'

How convenient would it be to be able to store for later what you have in access now? Like, between a freezing apartment where I can see my breath float up to my living room ceiling, and the stifling stuffy train car where I can hardly breath. Or, more deeply, the blessed, rambling, connecting conversations of an early dawn, and the later isolation. The stagnant work with ample time to relax, and the impending return to a rushed and stressed existence. And how convenient would it be to parse appreciation. Like when you look up at a jet stream in the late afternoon sky and your heart burns with love like the setting sun, but then, on an airplane much like the one you once longed for, which is taking you to one of the places you yearned for, and all you consider is whether you will make the connecting flight.

In these thoughts, then, I have resigned, if only for a moment, to the irreconcilable duality of body and soul, and found a strange solace in reminiscence. I have flown on an airplane and seen the spires of the Austrian Alps, but, then, I was hungry, and worried I would not have time for lunch in the Vienna airport. I have enjoyed a wonderful breakfast in the singing streets of my city, complete with a book and coffee and everything I could have expected to want, but, then, I worried over how I might explain my absence to the director of the organization I should've spent that morning with. Now, however, though in those moments I felt hot and cold, idle, and overstimulated, with time, my mind and body have overcome their differences to be painted over by the melancholy of nostalgia.

What will I next have too much of, then long for when it is gone? What is the next moment for me here? If it is good, will it be enough for me when it is not?

I'm sorry you're numbered among these deliberations,

Sam

11.

"Part of the work of being a modern person seems to be
dreaming of alternate lives in which you don't have to dream of
alternate lives. We long to stop longing, but we also wring
purpose from that desire."

Joshua Rothman

Dear Michelle,

We're in the same country.

I came home for my brother's wedding, and will be in St. Louis
less than a week. I know I promised you would be the first visit I
made when I returned to the US, and I hope you will not count
this against me. My trip is short, its nature demands I be with
family, and thus the significantly-reduced distance between us
remains impassable.

In consolation, this letter will at least reach you more quickly
than the others.

This homecoming was a surprise, in its occurrence and
circumstances. When I left for Ukraine, I made peace with the two
years. I've never been one to be homesick, and with so much to
experience on the opposite hemispheres, it felt shortsighted,
cowardly, even to spend time and money checking in on the places
I'd already been, the people I already knew. I imagine that's the
difference between wanderlust and a mature sense of wonder:
when you're young, it's easier to leave all behind. My brother's
marriage is a dramatic reminder life is not a novel. It continues,
even if I'm not involved. I want to see the world, but the people I
love are worlds within themselves, and there exists infinite
unexplored in both.

Kneeling aside my lifelong friend while he pledged his life to another was a depth of experience impossible for me to find on my own. I'm tempted to describe the moment as surreal, but am checked by the widespread overuse of the word, and its shortcomings. To generalize the memory by comparing it to a dream would be unfair to those I shared it with, and give too much power to dreams. Rather, the wedding, like much of my life since leaving you could be described as, was oversaturated. I feel distant from recent memory not because it was a dream, but because it was too real. Similar to the context overwhelming my interaction with my village baker, there was so much to every moment of this week's events it was impossible for me to purposefully engage with any of it. I lived, as I have so often been forced to in Ukraine, without thought, to the benefit of the moment and the detriment of its memory. When the past is a blur, I know, then, I was alive.

That his wedding coincided with my service was a compounding of the unknown, a second standard deviation from normalcy. From my former self. A dream within a dream, if I can briefly walk back on my earlier denunciation of surreal. To see my family, to be surrounded by those who are more real than anyone else, while simultaneously so far from familiar reality, led to a very strange inner encounter. I was looking into the mirrors of my loved one's gazes and did not recognize the person there, because they did not recognize him, either. I found some comfort in the role we all expected of each other, some cognition in the conventional dynamics which played out alongside the reunions, the bachelor party, the rehearsal dinner, the wedding mass, and the reception, and this was enough to hold onto to ensure the duality was distant, that I didn't collapse in on my confusion.

The ceremony was beautiful, by the way. I'm thrilled for and amazed by them both. Aside my inner journey, which seems to take precedence in every letter despite the inexhaustible external experiences they color, the beginning of their new life was a beautiful week for us all. To see someone whom I've known, loved, and aspired to my whole life definitively begin his own, with a person who knows him better than I could ever hope to, was singular, inspiring, and sobering in the implications of the wealth of individual experiences that existence is replete with. I am so amazed and grateful to have been brought into their joy for this time, as I'm sure could be said for all their guests. I am happy, and happy for them. It would be wrong to write of this week and not share this more meaningful, collective impression with you.

Perhaps it was the fleeting nature of this return, then, or the stark manifestation of an inner dichotomy, that I spent my quiet moments less on the differences between worlds and more on the person who existed within them, the differences between my selves, hurriedly reconciled after their reintroduction. American Sam met Ukrainian Sam, and in their tentative clash they immediately forgot how desperately I had longed for the ability to eavesdrop on a passing conversation, how badly I wanted to offhandedly comprehend everything the stranger in line for the bathroom said into his phone. I was, unfortunately, too intent on my own thoughts to listen to those of others.

What I am left with, what I received by forgoing the chance to reengage with the aspects of my home distance had indeed made me fonder of, was the particular realization that the progress in self-development I'd made abroad was perhaps more ephemeral than I'd thought. It was comforting, as I've mentioned, but simultaneously shocking and somewhat sad how quickly I reacclimated to my old roles, my abandoned habits, my former self. I had stepped into the person my loved ones took me for, my time apart from them unknown to them. What I had considered was true change was merely disillusionment, and I adjusted to how they saw me more quickly than I did to the time zone. This naturally led me to the grim inquiry: If my purpose in this endeavor was to better myself, would I have been better served focused solely the self whom I already knew, rather than form a new personality abroad, only to leave all of it behind when I came home?

Is the divide I feel really a difference at all? Is the language on the billboards and a long plane ride really enough to separate a human being?

A friend of mine told his partner, whom he met during our initial volunteer orientation, that, were it not for circumstance, he didn't think they would've become as serious as they had, as quickly as they did. While I am aware it was impossible for him to perfectly communicate what he was feeling, and certainly both myself, my friends, and most significantly, his girlfriend found it hard to reconcile what we understood with what he expressed, I think, after this trip, I better see his perspective. This life of ours is so variable, and is utterly defiant to our comprehension or control! That the program stipulates we exist in our new lives for 28 months, long enough to develop but absolute enough in its conclusion to call any such growth into question, that we exist in almost total isolation, that we are in the unknown and it will never truly become our own, was he wrong to say what he did? If his heart was swayed by situation, a context with an unflinching beginning and end, is he wrong to doubt whether he'd love her the same upon their return to the lives they left behind? Wouldn't those misgivings linger long after they've readjusted back to their home?? Can life be lived in the same manner, by the same person, who feels they are not?

* * *

Addressed on the desk in my Uzhhorodian apartment. I know I said I'd mail this from the states, but with so many lingering questions, I decided to wait until I had a more substantial closing thought. In the meantime, here are some things that happened to me, or the recollections which accompanied them.)

The world doesn't feel so vast when you fall asleep in a cabin and wake up in a new country.

Everything that happened in this fast and strange week culminated in an extended layover in Iceland, which I had booked the day before. For a soul seemingly outside of its life, there seemed no better place to reconnect, no place where I could more easily encounter myself. When I first faced that elemental wind, whipping off the unbroken coast and seizing me with awareness like I had dipped my head into the icy ocean itself, I knew my discord was shattered. The gale shattered what confusion I carried behind my eyes. I knew, instantly, I was there. The stinging cheeks and shivering bone left little disbelief.

I will forever cherish winter winds for the mindfulness they carry. Like a freezing shower, through shock, they ground.

Rejuvenated by the bitter, fresh air, forcing itself into my lungs with each bowed gasp, I explored Reykjavik, leaning against the furious gusts which tunneled through the city streets. At my hostel I helped an Australian exchange student with a puzzle, and later we ate fermented shark with a French au pair and a Spanish tourist. The four of us, bellies full of the repulsive dish and blood warmed by vodka as harsh as the land which cultivated it, then walked to the shore. A frigid mile from the city, adjacent a startlingly domestic neighborhood, stood a lighthouse. One of us had read this was the best place to see the Northern Lights without paying for a tour outside the city, and so the unlikely group huddled against a rock to hide from the spray while we waited, and became fast friends. We shared stories of warmer places under the infinite stars, as austere and magnificent as the country itself. Eventually, just as we were chased inland by the rising tide and pervasive chill, every part of us soaked and sure to be sick, a kind Icelandic man spotted us and escorted us to an alcove, laughing at our luck. Had we stayed at our perch for another hour, the water would've cut us off from the mainland.

He told us where to look, and upon the faintest glow of green above, we satisfyingly scampered home, for mulled wine and a promise to tell everyone we had seen the aurora in all its glory.

The next day, the receptionist, himself an expat from a far more temperate climate, convinced me on a group tour, and I boarded a van which took a small group of us south.

Along the way, while we passed digital street signs which displayed the current wind speeds, and the passenger Mercedes shook with the force, I looped Sigur Ros on my headphones, imagining no better musical accompaniment to the terrible beauty of the land we crossed than the otherworldly, echoing notes of the Icelandic group. What could better fit the uniqueness of the land than the art which was made upon it? From the window, and during the excursions outside, I saw the first snowfall of the season dust the early winter coats of the world's most resilient livestock, shared a freezing local yogurt outside a frozen gas station, visited the foot of the volcano which had famously halted Europe for weeks and consumed the former home of our tour guide, ate lamb stew in the highlands, euphorically embraced the black side of the southern shore as it pelted my raw skin, let the elements toss me back and forth like a child, absent the choice or thought to stand and fight, gleefully lets his parent toss him about, climbed a staircase of languages, encountering persons from across the globe who were all equally eager to summit the waterfall, and learned a simple truth: Nature is most beautiful when it is most dangerous.

Icelandic is (as far as I've been told) the only language in the world in which the word for nature is masculine. It is not hard to see why. The island is brutal, and whatever ingresses humanity can make into it are combative, and transient. Its ground is layered by the daily erosion, above are glaciers, below is the fire, the geothermal energy which powers much of the country's modern accoutrements.

I wrote a bad poem, which I will send along with this letter, with trembling fingers too excited by the day to consider the words themselves, and finally understood that while pictures and movies and songs and paintings inspire me to visit a place, its actual experience is never the same, and better for it. Were I to have felt like Daenerys when she walked the same shore, across the same black sand with those same black spires arising from the water beyond, I would have missed the bliss of being toppled by the wind for a passing sense of regal vengeance.

After this otherworldly encounter, whatever followed was sure to bring me crashing back down to Earth. This happened in dramatic fashion, in the form of several drunk Russian travelers who boarded the flight late and half of whom were eventually removed from the plane. By the time the ordeal was resolved an accepting grimace had spread across my face, and was cemented when the Turkish airport security randomly selected me for my 3rd stop and search of the trip when my electric toothbrush began buzzing as I shouldered my bag for the walkway.

I landed in the country with a heavy mind, and walked to the train station to deter any taxi driver from asking me why I was here.

I came here to chase the feeling of a thousand suns, I thought, back to the Linkin Park song of the same title. I thought, my luggage bouncing behind me, of a passionate teen in his first airplane listening to his favorite band's newest album, music imbued with just enough mysticism in its guitar and just enough angst in shaky vibrato which voiced the apocalyptic lyrics that it perfectly embodied his soul. Have you ever had a song fit a moment so entirely you felt it was sung to be heard exactly where you were? Or a movie mirror your life so wonderfully you can't help but return to it again and again, no matter how unsalvageable that nostalgia becomes? In this sense, they exists to help us experience. These twilight songs of a band past its prime were, this, then, inexplicably. Forever reminiscent of a trip to Italy he could hardly believe was happening, or appreciate in its own time: the music of an experience of a lifetime.

That night, I listened once more, desperate to recover their effect, despite knowing their reservoirs of emotional resonance had long since been depleted.

The night was soggy, the heavy clouds trapped the streetlights.

I ran away from something, to come here. Whether myself, decisions, or expectations. A year later, I found myself back in the US, and suddenly I was reticent to return? I thought I had what I needed from the experience, and learned on that long walk that my intentions had never been pure.

Why did I keep walking, then, if I had not come for the right reasons, and had returned devoid of even the wrong ones?

Then I saw an ancient cathedral, its illuminated black stone piercing the pressing night. I stopped.

Ukraine looked itself in the rain.

Reflection incited, I considered new starts, new things, new lives. What I had hoped to find here.

In this moment, I found, I believe, what was hereto inexorable, what made Ukraine so beautiful. This place is saturated with magic. The magic of the old, time-tested structures, culture, and people. The foundations of my experiences here have stood the test of time and been imbued by the consequences of this time. My first host family was an old woman, whose stories I never understood but who's eyes I did. The streets were uneven, but they were storied. This church was somber, but its effect on me had affected generations. The train cars creaked, but their sealed windows and peeling wood were the most thorough means by which I've ever escaped the world.

Here, time is respected. Here, I would say, the next time a cousin asks me at my brother's wedding why anyone would want to live here, Ukraine recognizes the nobility of that which has existed long enough to become old.

Of course, this attitude may be born largely of necessity, when the city doesn't have the budget for new busses, the busses which have transported for decades will continue to do so, and their charm will be felt only by those who do not ride them daily. Yet, perhaps, this necessity is a better angel of our human nature. Maybe we can only learn to appreciate the old when we are absent an easy replacement, when the passing relief of new is not so easily replenished, when things are not so easily replaced? Maybe necessity keeps things around long enough to survive the cycle of substitution, to survive novelty, normalcy, complacency, and the eventual urge to start over, so much so that the value it once enjoyed can be rekindled by nostalgia, contemplation, appreciation, the eventual revitalization of all which had value to be valuable again?

To clarify, at the foot of this dark tower, the timeworn newness of this place was apparent in the lack of any panicked need to arrive at the train station an hour before I boarded, and I knew then what I needed to bring home next time. I was not here for new experiences; they would not retain this nature. I was here for the true idea within the thousand suns, to experience by happenstance what would affect me for a lifetime, that which is original originally and appreciated in, and by, time.

When my service is over I want to return with a full journal, a gratitude for the years, some number of successful projects, and a fluency in Ukrainian. More significantly, however, I want to know what it is like to appreciate life for what it is, and discover this appreciation in more than the unusual.

I know you must be happy to read this. Looking back on our conversations, I understand that it's a sentiment you've always known I needed.

Ukraine looks itself in the rain, Michelle. I hope you know what I mean.

Renewed,

Sam

Windblown (Something Like a Poem).

These thoughts were typed into a frozen phone by numb fingers, whose errors have since been corrected,
On the black sand beaches of Iceland, where nature is awake.

Brace yourself.

Have you ever had your breath really taken away

Or do you just say breathtaking to sound pensive

Or because you have already overused incredible and amazing?

Sometimes I'll stand there

Facing the wind

The elemental power

Raw, my cheeks raw

It seizes me and with each gasp

Forces itself deeper into my lungs and soul.

I struggle to breath out

It is a labor

Which takes away everything else:

The roar in my ear shouts down terrible thought.

It whistles between the webs of my fingers, and tussles my hair like a wise friend.

This force is one of connection, bridging oceans and circumventing mountains, across the earth and all people.

When I suck in its gale I am breathing in the innumerable souls of this earth,

Each drinking from the same cup

And giving our own breath in return.

Where does the wind come from?

From the breath of billions.

The conversations,

the groans,

the sighs of relief,

the eruption of laughter and sobbing,

accumulating

Until that final push of air,

maybe it was a young child fighting up a hill on a rusty bike,

which sends the beautiful culmination on its journey.

I do not know who will feel it next.

I hope they turn into it and it takes their breath as well.

Whatever leaves you truly breathless is worth paying attention to.

Like dying, or wind.

Taste the wind whenever it finds you.

Can you feel my breath?

Can you taste the saltiness of windswept tears and sweat?

Can you feel the rain and snow and debris which fell but did not land, caught instead in the gale to then be flung across your face?

Can you feel the anxiety of an examination room which escaped when a door was cracked for air?

Can you feel the sharp punch of a sneeze, the short quick putters of a shiver?

Can you hear joy, exaltation, the sweet signing in showers and kitchens and concert halls, whistling tunes, shouts of triumph, the quiet conversations of old friends and the hurried and chaotic conversations of new ones?[14]

Can you know which breath you feel was the last someone else ever took?

Can you drink the humanity always in the breeze?

I hope you can.

Mine

and everyone's

whispers of love are carried in this wind.

Please, lean into it.

Lean into all of it.

---

[14] This of course being wind's biggest contributor, for who is more long winded than a person in a budding relationship?

12.

"We can never know what we want, because living only one life, we can neither compare it with our previous lives or perfect it in our lives to come.

Einmal ist keinmal"

Milan Kundera

Dear Michelle,

The most aspirational hopes of anyone who bade me a happy new year throughout the last holiday season have indeed been met. Whether they intended the sentiment, this first, full year in Ukraine has been one of the best of my life.

At least, upon reflection, this is what the impression of the totality of the year's experiences moves me to communicate. Perhaps the intensity of the moments with which these twelve months are imbued, the severity of the changes I underwent, the demands on my inner experience with which all memory is perceived, or, simply, that I had more cause to pay attention, this year was full, its recollection saturated, and this must be a good thing.

However, given the nature of many of these letters, the lengths I went to describe the difficulties of my time here, this summation feels wrong. Over-simplified. Easy. However, is it fair to let these struggles dominate dwelling? Surely, the hardships of this year are the more potent when remembered, painful memories command much more attention in contemplation than their pleasant counterparts. So, then, how can I arrive at an unbiased assessment of their sum total?

Perception is varied, more so than ever before on December 31st. The highs were higher. The lows were lower.

Can I say this year was, at once, the best and worst of my life?

You may, instead, ask me why I need to define the whole in the first place. But you know who I am, and you know my penchant for needless deliberation. Besides, how can I wish anyone a happy new year without first understanding what it is I'm wishing them?

Thus I elucidate, gazing out the small window of my hostel common room. I'm here to celebrate the new year with some friends, before my family arrives to see for themselves this place I've made my home. I've just finished a long conversation with a reputable Ukrainian journalist, who covers national events and who eagerly explained how the course of his country directly mirrored the path of the kingdom of Israel in the Bible's Old Testament. That he subsequently retired to a room of bunk beds shared between snoring teens and nocturnal tourists slightly discredited his self-proclaimed credentials. Cheap Christmas lights blink blue, red, and green in a corner near the untouched kitchenette, and an old vending machine hums its refrigeration behind a soft collection of Ukrainian carols. The effect of the room is contemplative, and I am grateful for it. I've found, when travelling, the most elusive encounters are those where the place I'm in complements the mood I'm in. Often one tends to subsume the other.

Tonight, though, I develop my personal tale of two cities. A year ago, I sat in a similar environment, a drafty hostel room in downtown L'viv I shared with a few volunteers. We were still in our beginnings, having reunited for the first time since dispersing throughout the country in October. We were in love with the newness, with each other, and with the romance of the cozy city square beyond our frosted windows. I had short hair then. One year hence and I am in Kyiv, a more bustling metropolis betraying a more notable Soviet influence, with its hardly-ordained facades and the striking murals which covered them. I am not in their room and not in love, yet there is so much about my present which replaces the happiness I felt last year.

My reassignment has brought immense joy, the overwhelming gratitude my partners have shown for the little efforts I've made in our short time together has filled me with something I was bereft of for nearly all my time in the village. And what a pleasure it has been to be less bound by the seasons! The stark absence of summer produce in the winter markets was initially charming, but after weeks of carrots and beets and cabbage, grocery store chains whose aisles offer spinach and blueberries year-round are gifts I will never again take for granted. While I miss the strength of the rural seasons, where fall and winter and spring and summer were a true life cycle one was obliged to participate in, where wilting and renewal were felt all the more intensely because of the more direct role nature had in our lives, a reliably-warm apartment and consistent bus schedules are a few of, in my humble opinion, life's bare necessities. I will likely never again know the atmosphere of an insular mountain community, where the isolation is tangible when the darkening nights are too cold for the long walk to the convenience store, and where the joy of spring is shared by all who buy their farm-fresh fruit in perfectly-ripened bulk, yet I am grateful I once did.

I write with optimism, then, with wonder for where I have come and will go. Maybe a year can only be judged by the emotions with which it ends. Akin to a life judged by its passing, the final moments of a man determinative of his legacy, tonight, I am happy, and, therefore, I must have lived a happy year. Today, I felt the sun melt my frozen lashes and waited as my once-suspended breath thawed and rolled down my cheeks like joyful tears shed for the blinding afternoon light, and this has been the best year of my life.

I have so much to look forward to, and so much to look back on. No matter the effect, an abundance of reality is a thing to be celebrated.

My hope for you, Michelle, is that your year be as consuming, overwhelming, volatile, unpredictable, and replete with memory as mine has been, and, in this, you will know an abundantly happy New Year. So, Happy New Year. Or, rather, I hope your new year is happy. The former just sounds demanding.

Should old acquaintance be forgot, and in an effort not to be,

Sam

13.

"For I have learned
To look on nature, not as in the hour
Of thoughtless youth; but hearing oftentimes
The still sad music of humanity,
Nor harsh nor grating, though of ample power
To chasten and subdue."

William Wordsworth

Dear Michelle,

Something I've thought a lot about while writing you these stories is whether any of them will continue to play a role in my life. When the strict two years are over, which memories will remain? What will I most miss when I am thinking about you from the other side?

As a child, I never chose what I was going to be nostalgic for. When I plucked out a collection of Calvin and Hobbes from the sparse shelves of my grade school library, the one under the stairs at the small Catholic school in that small town, which doubled as the music room and was the scene of a daily discord between the soft spoken librarian and the screeching ear needles of poorly-played plastic recorders, I was entirely unaware of how much I would come to love those cartoon characters, and that little room for introducing us. An act as insignificant as the free-reading periods themselves, a choice as haphazard as any of the infinite I've made since I was able to, brought me a foundational aspect of my childhood. From then on, the three of us were inseparable. As you well know, I still keep them with me, wherever I go. Currently, in the other room sits one of the several volumes I purchased that night after our conversation, in spite of my budget and recent insistence I didn't need a copy while in college.

When I sat down to start this letter last night, I felt a sudden urge to reunite with the characters, their accompanying recollections, which I realized I hadn't revisited since I repacked my checked bags at their initial weigh-in in Washington. I soon lost myself in the greyscale strips, running through those nondescript forests with that little rascal and his beloved tiger, far from our vexed parents. I'd missed them more than I had expected to.

Now, having binged on nostalgia and rendered rational once more by the morning and an oily French press, I know what I truly miss is who I was when I first met them. Their antics are dormant neural pathways of my childhood wonder, their smiles remind me of my own abandoning playfulness, their images reflective of the heavy-threaded experiential tapestry of childhood. Their stories, my memories, seized upon my imagination like Hobbes pummeling Calvin when the front door opens and he's home from school. I felt similarly tackled by the sinking dread time might make us strangers. I spent the night firmly transfixed to, by, a happy heartache.

The rare feeling of rediscovered joy, of which nostalgia is a mere harbinger, is terrifying to release, once found. How many more times will these Sunday paper friends bring me back? I doubt I'll revisit them for some time; I am desperate not to dilute their effect.

Instead, this morning, I wonder with you.

What of today will be similarly remembered tomorrow? What experiences, conscious or accidental, will affect me so consequentially, will seize me so strongly they remain significant to who I am a decade from now? I wish, I know, Auschwitz will.[15]

My family came to visit me.

My parents and two of the brothers arrived a few weeks ago. From the time I met them at their Airbnb, a Kyiv high-rise unlike anything I'd known existed in this country, I remembered the

---

[15] That is, provided my efforts to remember do not diminish the likelihood I will, much like another family vacation, this to Florida, which presently exists in my mind only as the paralyzing sunburn I came home with.

wedding. Seeing them, again, as a person wholly different from who I was when I left them, but absent any understanding of these changes which had occurred while I was so far from them, I felt my mind ushered back to that middle. That haunting in-between, the sensation I first encountered when I was first home and seen by them for the first time and described to you in sufficient detail and insufficient clarity. Reminded of this feeling, I am reminded of your response. You were right.

Inherent to our friendship, the foundation of our connection, is the knowledge you've asked of yourself the same question which echoed in the frozen streets as our group sight-saw them: am I real to them, or to myself?

Their realities are far too distinct for they both to exist.

At the crux of this disparity is where I call home. Is it this place they had come to visit, is it where they came from, or is it wherever we are? Coming home, to be reflected by the eyes of a loved one, from a place you call home which means nothing to them, is the strangest sensation of a transient life. Allowing for, reestablishing with the old, once you've accepted the new, seems to rend the soul.

I had hoped having them here would mend the divide, solder my present to my past, reconcile the disconnect which permeated my return to the States. I had hoped, in seeing the landmarks of my old life aside the landmarks of my new one, my family below the grey monuments and their own impressions of the challenging cuisine, would bring together my persons.

I remain, however, disparate. In Ukraine, and so far and away from who I left behind.

Thus, our time here, in Poland, and in Germany were brief. The excitement of those moments superseded any need to engage with them, the abundance of moments superseded any need to choose them, the incessance of moments superseded any need to reflect on them, until, much as I was in the St. Louis airport, I rode the commuter train through the German countryside dumbstruck by the immense scope of experiences my mind had fused. The late sun in my fatherland bathed the baffled expression of a tourist whose trip could only be recalled and then later described as a blur. Indistinct were the museums, the Cuban-themed New Year's celebration in Krakow, the surfer on a Munich canal, the pretzels and perogies and borsch and beer and beer and beer, the thousand looks of the communal panic of mutually late passengers, the churches, the smiles, the arguments, the pictures, the landscapes, the faces of awe and exhaustion, the coffee, the hotel sheets, the concerts, the Geiger counters, the bus rides, the underground salt figures, the tour group lunches, and all the more indistinct aspects of normalcy on pause: It was as if they had been uploaded, that my mind was an online album, that its multitude of recent incredible memory a collection.

All, save Auschwitz.

Before I continue to the heart of this letter, though, for whatever tropes follow, forgive me. Aware of your family's and my own's connections to this place, I tried tirelessly to write this story with the gravitas such a space deserved. This effort has been paralyzing. Self-doubt is sown between the blank spaces, and if I fill them with words that have already been used, illustrate impressions that have already been described, I feel I am disrespecting what Auschwitz is for all those who have passed there or passed through. Passion is a platitude for a place so powerful. Yet, absent passion, I cannot properly relate what it was like to be there. After a seemingly infinite number of scrapped copies beside me, I accept at last that what I say may well have been said, and what I felt will surely have been felt, before and again. Perhaps this is why these horrors are preserved: that we may recognize our shared humanity in our shared experience. The entry fee is empathy.

Thus, to say that I have been singularly affected by this place seems either the single most awful aggrandizement of my ego, or the single most banal summation I've ever made. It is, however, all I can say. I was singularly affected by Auschwitz, as has anyone who has ever been there, or will ever be.

To explicate the effect would be to rob it of its power. Words are of little use to a singularly heavy heart.

So, then, what can I tell you about this place? Without an emotion to elucidate, what can I describe that you couldn't find in a Google image search? The memorials are just another tourist attraction, after all, well-documented by individuals far more adept at this than I. The fledging, oft-ignored writer within, aimless without the emotive impetus, wants me to build the setting, to describe for you in great detail the throngs of people outside the gates, the empty board houses lined in neat rows and bathed in the melancholy of a winter afternoon's sun, the crunch of the gravel between prison barracks and gallows, between gas chambers and furnaces? Where would that bring you, though, if I simply set the scene? To history books, I imagine. To documentaries. To The Boy in the Striped Pajamas, The Band of Brothers. To representation.

Why, then, did I go? To gather my own impressions, and later, offer an image of this place indecipherable from previous depictions? If these were my motivations, I would have been wasting my time.

I've always said that I don't like to take pictures of famous places. Such oft and well-photographed locale will, inevitably, have been rendered far more beautifully than I could ever aspire to, with my iPhone and eye for only the most lowbrow principles of photography. I prefer, rather, to capture these places within my time, in such a way as to denote what they were to me when I saw them, singular in the context of my singular experience. A monument predates me, and will outlive me, and I include in its picture the old man sitting beside it, because that is how I encountered it. No one else, for its timeless existence, will ever witness it in the same light, ever view it with my limited perspective and brief context, no one else will remember it and see the old man situated below, like so. That's what I want form a photo. An image of my unique encounter, for me, a memory, for everyone else, a moment unlike anything they have in their own albums.

The same goes for Auschwitz-Birkenau, rendered in words, not pixels. Its stories written, told, recollected, or spoken, are innumerable. They grow exponentially, multiplying with every visit and generation, dependent upon the needs of the world to be reminded of its deepest scars. Such is the power of this place, the weight of its memories, the burden on our collective unconscious.

How, then, could I, with my inherent limitations attendant to my four hour tour, five hours of sleep, my distractions: the location of the nearest bathroom, whether the cute girl in the other tour group notices me, the drip of my runny nose, and how I can most effectively force my mind to ignore these and the thousand other distractions that flesh is heir to and remain with my present, so as to be most significantly impacted by what ought to be a life-changingly devastating experience, how could I, considering, hope to describe this place in a way those who lived, suffered, or died here, or told the story of those who lived, suffered, or died here, have not previously achieved? Even if I could, my impressions would be unworthy. I entreat you to read the testimonies of the victims of the Holocaust, seek one out before they are only memory, watch a cinematic interpretation of its horrors, or visit a museum to see its terrible artifacts and envision them for yourself.

Bear in mind, though. Nothing, not even physical or mental presence, will prepare you for the depth of its effect, should you be fortunate enough to know it. Therefore, I will spare you any attempt at giving you what you ought to give yourself.

What I can say for my presence, for the throngs of people waiting their turn to willingly enter those evil-wrought gates, and must first make clear, was the horrifying sensation of walking with eagerness in buzzing groups and in the steps of those who once trod with paralyzing dread. This dichotomy was most apparent in the images we took of the images we saw.

Those whose eyes are wide in black and white are eyes widened by fear, those whose eyes are wide in color are eyes widened by what had happened here.

This somber oddness escalated to near self-hatred when I turned my camera towards "Arbeit Macht Frei"[16], and, upon the closing shutter, snapped out of my inquisitive trance, my desire to see what lay beyond the gate, and remembered that years ago a young man much like me had this image engrained in his resolutely hopeful mind while he took the last steps he ever would outside of

---

[16] "Work Makes One Free"

those walls. Similar in age, in appearance, in dreams, myself anxious to enter, him, anxious to die.

From then on, every step my shame accrued. My phone remained in my pocket. What I can recall without guilt are fleeting observations. The barracks are no longer empty. They are filled by tourists, signs, maps, prints, and pounds and pounds and pounds of shoes and clothes and kitchenware and toys and teeth and sweat and dirt and pain, of fists pounding floorboards and arched backs naked against cryptic walls, and dried tears, a century old and fresh. The sound of the gravel which is laid between them is not the comfort of a country road but macabre, the visceral grating of rope around spine, skeletal aching of malnourished joints, now, rubber of my Nike's against the dusty stone.

When I kicked one of these rocks, a habit I'd formed when the boarding school's mandatory daily prayer walks left me with nothing to do but focus my attention on a unique object and try to bring it along with me in stride, I reencountered the young man, both of us now behind the walls. Through his eyes, I kept, as we all are wont to do, putting myself here. With his experience in mind, I considered, the horrid reality of my theories would set in soon, that I would have found a way to escape. That I would have survived. Surely, a resourceful, smart young man would be among those who were rescued. This assurance was justified in my experiences: I'm resourceful, adaptable, I blend in easily, and people generally like me. Maybe I would've lasted, biding my time, kicking rocks until we were set free.

Then I walked into another barrack, through another hallway, and ran my hand along the glass which separated me from a formless mound of human hair.

In the sight of this grotesque memorial, I saw my self-assurances for the lies they were, and the comfort of my delusional invincibility was shattered. The most terrible insight gripped my heart. The bastion of hope I read into every story of human demise, which I allowed myself to feel whenever I encountered death, which always reminded me my story would be ongoing, wilted in this vile place. Only then did the full scope of the atrocities committed here fall upon me. The weight of 6 million lives ladened my pace and I slunk behind my tour group.

My ability to get others to like me, my unassuming personality, any advantageous aspect of my person, my individuality itself, would have meant nothing here. The most likeable cattle are still slaughtered.

Accepting my insignificance, then, how could I live in view of so many lives who never had a chance, when I understand that all which distinguishes us is chance? Where do I go, with this young man in tow?

I cried for him, for others, and for my own chastened luck, careful not to let my siblings see.

From Auschwitz we took a silent bus to Birkenau, that great and sprawling state park of misery.

That lush, open land is the archetype of juxtaposition. Without the gates, the tracks, the ashes, the tombstones, the crumbling remains of temporary holding areas, for so many, the last and pathetic place they called home, without the words "For ever let this place be a cry of despair and a warning to humanity, where the Nazis murdered about one and a half million men, women, and children, mainly Jews from various countries of Europe" cemented in every language of Europe below a haunting spectacle of dark, immovable, abstract form, and beside the haunting simplicity of the pit where once humans were eradicated on schedule, without the lives you can taste in the wind, when the breeze whips through the silent pastures and carries with it agony, this place would be a beautiful ruin: a scenic, sweeping plain intermixed with romantically dilapidated structures. Testaments to a simpler time. Perhaps William Wordsworth would've composed a few lines beside Auschwitz-Birkenau.

When we left, the sun was fading, and my brothers and I sought refuge in passing conversation. Behind us was something we did not want to take with us and always would. In that moment, however, it was all I could do to turn around. When I did, I was frozen, a pillar of salt and sorrow. Hereafter, if I ever wish to sound poetic, and can bring myself to voice it, I'll say I saw a spectacular sunset over Auschwitz.

Heavily,

Sam

14.

"It is forgetting about things* that renews their wonder"

Alan Watts

Dear Michelle,

The collection in my notes which contain excerpts from stories yet unwritten often have a life of their own. For example, some snippets of dialogue, character development I promise to eventually include in a story about a divorced man who starts to find his midnight world so preferable to his reality that he starts to seek out lucid dreaming methods, now reads as if I'd written it for myself. In one of these conversations, the man's therapist tells him, upon a perceived breakthrough in his relationship with his daughter:

"Now that you are awake again, regard the waking world as you did the dream."

Their conversation continues and its relevancy is diluted by requisite long-windedness, but its initial message reads as potently for my present mind as I hope it will for the novel's readers, if it ever comes to fruition.

When you start the year in the remnants of a concentration camp, it, as I have communicated, is nearly impossible not to feel as if you've been awakened. The experience is epochal, and though unconfirmed by experience, I trust I'm not the only one who considers a pre and post-Auschwitz era in their annals of memory. The angry wind that forces its way through the cracks in those buildings culpable in that greatest of human atrocities is fiercer than any coastal breeze, more powerful than any maelstrom, and more awakening than any breath, absent the first. I do not know how long the effects will last, but I write them down under the guise of relating them and in the hopes of preserving them.

Simultaneously, though, when you spend New Year's Day in the remnants of a concentration camp, it can be difficult to be excited for the 364 ahead. The joys of life are illuminated, but this same awakening renders the discomforts of daily existence acerbic, observed by the engaged mind in their entirety and made all the more painful for their insignificance in light of the horrors some have faced in their own lives.

Thus, any holocaust tourist returns with a dilemma: to embrace, or release, the experience. To release, to be relieved from the torments of compared suffering, to embrace, to welcome the necessity of making the most of one's life, while welcoming the aggravated disappointment when one inevitably fails to consistently do so. The discord is akin to a New Year's resolution, ironically. A more rewarding life is sought, the fulfillment of a purpose is perceived and savored, but, in view of these goals, one's accepted shortcomings are passive no longer. What was dormant demands attention, and the status quo of a day ago becomes a failure to act.

Choosing to be numbered among the latter, to hold the lost life in my heart and let the souls of the perished guide me to a more complete reality, I needed to find the joy quickly, and seize upon it with the ferocity of one whose days are numbered in days. The best I can describe the sensation, for myself, and for you, Michelle, is that I feel like I've received a briefly terminal diagnosis. For a moment, I glanced through the eyes of someone who knew death was soon for them, and since, happiness has been my aim, and my mistakes are excruciatingly wasted time. I wonder how anyone with weeks to live is able to spend any of that time asleep. My laziness will never be more poignant than on my deathbed.

Gratefully, I did not go home immediately after Poland, and the rest of the time away from home brought me an immense joy which has spilled over into my daily life in Ukraine. Still, though I arrived in that humble apartment and stagnant workplace I said goodbye to last year, I have kept with me the gratitude that Auschwitz gave me, the exaltation of a spring morning in the bleak midwinter. For now, I consider everything in my life as brighter, and with greater patience. My faults are felt more critically, but my successes are more fruitful, my contentment more replete than it has ever been since my visa was stamped. Reflecting on this levity, and having finally rediscovered the simple wonder of routine, waking with bad coffee and a plodding manuscript, hopscotching puddles on my path to the office, biding my time with simple acts of usefulness which barely fill an afternoon, awaiting the days when I have my youth clubs, I sense the urge to write, and have the chance to tell you about those most recent international adventures. I hope that in recounting their joy it will be available, however second-handedly, to you.

From Krakow, my family and I travelled to Germany. We went, less to experience, and more to see.

Initially, my parents planned this trip for a sense of why I'd chosen to make a home so far away from their own. They came to better understand me, and through me, this country. Given its incidental proximity to our inherited homeland and wondering if they'd ever step foot in this part of the world again, our visit to Poland became a necessity. Why, then, did we go to Munich?

Of course, my father is German, but his roots have long since sprouted, digging deep into Midwest farmland. My mother's, more recently transplanted, have yet to truly take hold in the soil of the States. The concrete is hard in Chicago, and she grew up in a Polish America, not as American from Poland. Thus, throughout my childhood, her cultural heritage played to much greater effect, even if its outward expressions were limited mostly to Polka and perogies. Being in Poland, therefore, felt much more a return than I expect to experience in any other foreign country. I learned there a little more of who I am when I say family. What I learned in Germany was that discovery is not a part of this world.

What I mean is that there is little on this planet which has yet to be glimpsed by some human eyes. And since everything is seen, we need to see everything for ourselves. With no great and distant lands awaiting our exploration, the closest we can achieve to that indescribable relief of the barrelman's "land ho", as his eyes land on undiscovered earth, to see it all with our own. To search for it on a screen, then compare the impression it leaves in reality to what we expected from the photos.

For reality's part, and modernity's sake, seeing it for yourself welcomes enough of the unknown to make the journey worthwhile. Absent the deeper meaning of ancestral connection or the power of a place imbued by the presence of our loved ones, there is still so much to see. And, maybe, that's the point.

What I saw, for example, in Budapest, was an apartment nestled above a gentleman's club on the crest of the hill where once the leaders of the Austro-Hungarian Empire planned the unification of the cities of Buda and Pest, which soldiers of the Ottoman Empire once climbed in their ultimate, conquering steps, and where before them, nearly a millennia ago, Mongols made the same victorious surmount. This apartment had a fuse box that was impossible to find, and, coupled with the Airbnb check-in instructions, I felt like an accomplished Sherlock Holmes by the time I felt the cool, conditioned air inside. That night, I learned strip clubs make for lousy downstairs neighbors.

Encouraged by the steady bass reverberating beneath me, I became a nocturnal tourist, reveling in the city's warm glimmer from high above the Danube, the spectacularly ancient landmarks glowing like galaxies dotting the dark hills they sat on. Further, in historic Buda, I laid down on the steps of the iconic Hungarian Parliament building, the most photographed structure for hundreds of miles, and watched the sparrows which roost in its domes swim in the black sea of a starless night against the amber sky. They reminded me of the water bugs from my childhood, darting endlessly without an apparent purpose or pattern, mesmerizing.

In the daylight, I saw the heartbreaking remains of my first cup of Starbucks coffee in a year and a half seeping into medieval concrete, and the humorous glances stolen at the heartbroken foreigner who had spilled his drink seconds after purchasing it. I saw the Sziget festival, a frenzied display of color and frivolity and experience, the beauty of a hundred countries represented by the thousands of their citizens who had gathered on this little island to gather the rosebuds of youth. I saw the ecstatic joy of community sour into the madness of a mob when the night's headliner took the stage and the crowds pressed closer. In those currents of chaos I was swept into a group of Irish visitors whose chants of "F*** Ed Sheeran" had an inexplicably calming and comforting effect, then colliding with a man from France far too intoxicated to care, and a gaggle of Englishmen who were holding back the tides so a daughter could enjoy the concert undisturbed from her father's shoulders. I locked arms with their group, and later we toasted our heroics with boozy slushies and danced until the sun came up.

In the hazy aftermath of that euphoric festival, I cried in the coolest bar I'd ever been in, filled with a searing longing to remain in this beautiful place, and saw the powerful beam of a border guard's flashlight pierce my eyelids for the 3am crossing inspection. Over the next two hours, I learned that the European Union had been outfitted with the latest in train track technology, while Ukrainian railways still relied on outdated fittings. Any train which travelled both had to make the cumbersome transition before crossing over, and, with exhaustion's frustration mounting, I cursed the arbitrary nature of the world's self-imposed boundaries. I have never desired international unity more deeply than when the dissolving of state lines directly coincided with my ability to sleep.

What I saw in my Vienna layover, and what I described at greater, more narrative length in the short story I included with this letter[17], came into sharp relief the moment I thought I'd ordered a water with my dinner and the waiter brought a bottle of Beefeater 24 with my chicken sandwich. Having begun the day with a pot of coffee 8x too large for my physique because I was at one of the most famous cafes in a city famous for its cafes and I had chosen a menu item based on a presupposed notion of how expensive the coffee would be, the face to face with a full bottle of liquor sent my physical and financial heart into a panicked pulse. With the contrasting stimulants fighting for supremacy and most of my budget already allocated, I attended a concert in the most illustrious venue in all of Vienna, sitting bug-eyed behind world-

---

[17] Before My Own Sunrise, also available here: www.samuel-gerard.com/samuel-gerard/before-my-own-sunrise

renowned performers dressed in period piece. Their renditions of classic compositions, written in this very place, were otherworldly, and I was transported to a time of when the banks of a blue Danube could still be enjoyed within city limits. Or maybe it was the caffeine, alcohol, and extreme self-consciousness elicited by my seat on stage and in full view of the hundreds of Asian tourists in attendance which brought me to another time. In either case, it was a supernatural evening. Determined to reenact the events of my then favorite film, Before Sunrise, which I had watched twice in anticipation of this trip, I bought a street-side espresso and 6 hours with a city bike, and I pedaled until my heart and soul were sure to burst with the beauty of a silent Austrian midnight and with the exertion it took to navigate its winding alleys and cobbled streets. I saw too much to sleep, though I saw little which noticed me. The conversation I did have, the sunrise bunk chat with me, Earl, and the dying woman who shared our hostel room, might have easily been a hallucination at that point in the night. Regardless of its reality, it seemed I was destined to live out a different movie, one more tragically romantic than I ever could have possibly hoped for.

What I saw on my way back to Ukraine was a car, whose seats I shared with a traveling New England Methodist and two friends making some extra cash by peddling international travelers, broken down at a Shell station in Hungary. Unfortunately for the minister I hadn't slept a wink the night before, and the lulling argument of the pseudo-mechanics, standing over the ajar engine block, proved more compelling than a discussion of the Ukrainian Christian mission. I awoke on the road again, more specifically, the road's shoulder, because the vehicle's owner had concluded the only way were getting back to Ukraine intact was if he kept the speedometer under 40 km/h, with my backseat companion indignant that I had fallen asleep in the middle of his life story. I saw how poorly timed my decision was to experience what falling asleep in front of someone actively engaged in a dialogue with me, because the eight-hour trip which should've only been four passed in an uncomfortably deliberate and slow silence.

What I saw on my last afternoon in Munich, at a small Thai restaurant where I had stopped for lunch, was a young couple crying into each other. I wanted so badly to afford them the privacy their moment deserved, yet I could not keep my eyes from the power behind their faces. Faced with such raw, tender emotion, each of us in that tiny space were subtly transfixed by their grief. I saw her move over to his side of their window-side booth. I saw them hold each other, desperately, as if, if either of them relaxed their grip, their lives would slip away. I saw, in glimpses, the strength they were trying to project to the other. Maybe they had come here to have their difficult conversation in a public and quiet place so they could more easily feign this strength, so they might be encouraged, by the certainty of onlookers, to refrain from weeping, or spilling more than they felt necessary to communicate what they must. Between bites of food, whose taste I had no awareness for and whose function had lost all significance, I watched as they cried, then, silently, and without warning, stood up and left. One of them glanced behind her, to see the place which would loom so large in her near future, and in her trailing contemplation I caught her gaze, and I felt myself shatter. Then a younger, happier couple replaced them, and I lost the two terrible figures as they walked together and apart, to the right and the river.

In telling you this, more so than anything else I've related in these letters, I have coopted their story, their precious moment, and I wonder if I am at all worthy of retelling it. The indescribable experience of utter sorrow rendered into a sloppy paragraph by an outside observer. Can a stranger's words ever encapsulate what it was like to really live? I guess that is the work of an artist. To tell stories they cannot not know. Of course, this led me to reconsider the question of my future, to rekindle the long-dormant debate over what I might do next. These, however, are reflections for another time. They are not what I saw.

What I saw when I came home was how fortunate I am to be here. In the end, that's what I always see best when I travel, and what we all must be chasing in the wanderlust. We misplace our wonder, stepping outside our worlds help us to see what is wonderful is what we leave behind. I see my home for what it is, my norm for its wonders. When you rely on something different to be something special, you are sure to miss the beauty of everyday life.

Beauties like volunteering for a local English summer camp and showing up with one pair of underwear and discovering it's a week-long, sleepaway bike trip with a deeply religious bent, the kind that required I ask permission of my Peace Corps supervisor to attend and the kind she'd be required to tell me I could not attend because of the Peace Corp's emphasis we keep our work strictly secular. Like conversations with my English club kids and being asked with sincere innocence: "Where were you made?", or told, with sincere flattery: "You have eyes like a cow." From potholes and potatoes to creme brule's in a faux-French café, the beauties of each day are bountiful.

Looking forward,

Sam

P.S.: You've asked about my more creative writing, and I admit I've been lax about keeping up with any work I'm comfortable sharing. In my mind, if the inspiration which spurs the story is strong enough for me to finish it, then it must have been something I needed to tell, and something I need to share. Recently, this has happened only once. I was in Vienna, visiting on the implicit recommendation of a favorite film's filming location, as I often do, provided they were shot in accessible destinations. When I came home, a night, borrowing heavily from the movie which initially sent me to the city, came into focus, and, though I lacked the creative energy to give my character a new name, what I've included in this envelope is the closest I've come to fiction with any semblance of foundation.

Before My Own Sunrise.

While planning a trip to Vienna, a young man and aspiring cinephile watches Before Sunrise, an idealism starring Ethan Hawke and Julie Delpy. The movie, which he adores, presents him with a drastically inflated perception of the city's romance in a place already intoxicatingly, perhaps dangerously, fanciful. Convinced the setting will produce for him a similar idyll, he travels there for a sleepless night of pre-determined consequence.

What follows is an increasingly tired (and unedited) narration.

18:30

I walk from my third floor hostel to the concert hall dressed in the most formal attire of my backpack wardrobe, i.e. a wrinkled second-hand linen jacket and the bleached chinos.

The streets are hazy, and I hope the afternoon rain spent these low clouds. I have a long way to walk.

There is a large market across the street, and I begin my journey there, on the narrow walkway between the wooden booths. They are already boarded and block the historic and place setting cast iron streetlamps, but the light slipping from the few quiet restaurants tucked between souvenir shops and seafood vendors is enough to get by on, and the shadowed brick escorts me through. A chalkboard in a bar window advertises 2-1 gin and tonics until 8 and there is a sizable and young crowd inside, but I have an endless night ahead of me and don't want to miss its beginning.

Besides, I think, it's too cliché for my companion to be waiting for me in a bar.

19:00

The Musikverein, the timeless venue, the captured sounds of innumerable modified breath through pristine brass and taught strings still reverberating across the glassy tile and between marble pillars and behind the painting frames. It is well and truly breathtaking and has continued to render me speechless. How could I possibly do justice to such opulence?

I am set to pose this question to the friendly receptionist, but a large tour bus has just unloaded, and he sends me and my ticket quickly off with a smile.

A woman reads my ticket with a confused look and ushers me behind the stage, where I sit among my much more presentable peers.

The crowd's din quiets in anticipation and the artists enter the stage with quiet confidence, the scene is set for their daily and our grand event.

By some miracle mishap booking I am seated just behind these musicians. They wear the garb traditional to Mozart's time and their powdered wigs bounce while they finish tuning. Then the conductor with a conductor's strut takes the podium, raises a crooked and resolute right hand, and they launch directly into their exquisite ensemble.

After the encompassing sound purges me of my distractions, be it my attire or desire to make the most of this experience, I close my eyes and I drift with the legacy of the music. The sweeping melodies bring me to old Vienna, a place and time when their composer walked the same sculpted, now-storied, streets, when this creative savant transcribed his world into the music bound to outlast even humanity itself.

His music is almost enough to satisfy my greater purpose. Why wander empty streets when I have already discovered profound beauty, a moment for a lifetime?

And yet, as I dared to open my eyes, scanning the scores of enchanted gazes fixated on those performers before me, I am reminded of the intensity of more tangible romance, the passion I seek tonight which any art can only ever reflect, by a girl in the box three from the left.

19:30

She wore a white shawl wrapped around a black dress that would impress any room, and its effects were the more pronounced as it were so perfectly suited to the opulence of this concert hall, and was juxtaposed by the casual attire of the general audience beneath her. Around her graceful neck a chain of gold shone under the crystal chandeliers like the adorned nymphic pillars. Her hair was styled nonchalance, dark locks draping across her forehead and hanging with the enticing possibility of falling from their place. Her hands were resting on a covered left knee as if Tolstoy himself was instructing her posture.

Her expression of casual allure, exclusive to those fortunate few all too aware of their own elegance, was reflected in the faces of the Greek gods looking down from their oily heavens, and in the gilded sheath and flowering ornaments which surrounded us all.

She sat perfectly still, in every sense of the word. This was, moreover, not the stillness of cursory observation, either, because for some time now my eyes had not strayed from contemplation of her. Her face was turned towards me yet far enough away to remain indistinct. Perhaps she was trying to stay awake, perhaps she knew better than to watch the movement of the performance, or perhaps, her eyes were meeting mine in that brilliant room.

The music swelled with my beating heart and racing imagination, and her distant face became the nexus of all the grace available in those sights and sounds. Deft hands worked precious instruments and we strained to catch their every note, and I saw her, though at that time I felt this burgeoning infatuation an unfortunate distraction inhibiting the other wonders present, but later I was grateful my attention was thusly held, as hers was the sole figure who still belonged in the idealized scene which would soon play in my memory.

I unwittingly brought my left hand to my face and played a finger across my lips, letting the music glide my thumb and forefinger along its surface, letting a sharp crescendo pinch the place where it had chapped. Was she alone, a patroness of the splendor she embodied? Was she with her parents, had they dragged her from some more illustrious or engaging engagement?

Then the score dropped. Did she speak English? Would she permit any advance, let alone mine?

She brought a hand to her face as I had moments before, and the tempo intensified. After we both turned our heads, I let myself wonder if she might be mimicking my movements, if I had her mind as she held mine and the symphony crescendo-ed.

Accelerando.

The symbols thunder!

I am in my childhood home again, looking up from my Capri Sun to confusingly admire the cartoon character with wide eyes who blushed bright red when she smiled.

The drums boom!

I am holding a soft hand in my parents' basement and my eyes are firmly fixed on the forgotten film.

The brass peal!

I am a nervous sophomore at the Cheesecake Factory with the friend of my friend whose friend told me about her friend who liked me.

The strings and woodwinds resound!

I am kissing, or kissed, under moonlight on a cold fall night while the others waited in the parking lot.

The hall was respite with sound and my mind with imagination, and the orchestra resonated wondrously the recollection of these youthful romances!

21:00

When the final echoes of applause calmed, the audience paused a collected pause. The music was over, and the fantasies it wrought receded. Then the murmurs began again, this time full of appreciation and logistics.

Those between us stirred, quickly becoming a throng, but I waited, as did she. I sensed her delay an invitation and this was worrying as I did not know what it might be for. So I stood transfixed, imploring my legs to move, to take the stairs to where she waited, and yet before they could oblige, a nearby usher bade an over-excited visitor to vacate the first violinist's chair and while the confrontation had my attention the girl in the box disappeared into the hall.

Then, with the possibility our rendezvous might prove impossible, my legs of course set off in a panic. I had to meet her now that it was not a guarantee I do so.

In the foyer the grateful assemblage clustered, took pictures, and said their goodbyes. I scoured them for a glimpse of that white shawl and nervously whistled The Waltz of the Blue Danube, ever more certain that she had eluded me.

21:30

Outside the magnificent façade of the concert hall shone like a baroque moon, bathing the square in the soft light reflected from its luminous stone. More pictures were taken, and I strode through the backgrounds to no avail.

Soon, the cover of numbers dispersed, my hope was spent, and the one and young family who remained began to send more frequent and inquisitive looks in my direction. I was forced to abandon my search and move on.

Unsure of my next act, and like one rising from too long a nap needing to process the nonevent which had so vividly lived in my mind, I ducked into an alley to give myself some time to think. It was between the dark and ornate residential facades where I realized, with a slight twinge of panic, that I had already exhausted all my plans. All night is quite a long time, I chided myself.

With nothing else to do, I began my wandering sooner than I had expected to, sad for what might've been and a greatly relieved it had stayed just that.

The alley, or, more fittingly, a silent side street, took me to another of the picturesque Vienna squares, which, it seemed, the city was in no short supply of. Golden light of wrought buildings hung over storefronts of dazzling glamour and leading fashion. Their spotless windows held the judging gaze of flawless plastic mannequins, whose shiny black skin looked as if it were hewn from the carpet of cloudless night which wound with the throughway, accentuating its brilliance.

Walking along this illustrious ravine, I followed the general buzz of activity to the city's center, where nearly the entirety of the still-active Venetians and its tourists had congregated.

The avenue was almost impossibly glamorous, lined with stores I could hardly afford to window shop at and restaurants and cafes brimming with the Saturday evening.

Near one of these bustling patios was a stone fountain which looked tragically commonplace in the setting, and I felt it as good a place as any to sit and reflect. The cool stone was smooth and damp, and I promptly busied myself with the lives that passed before me.

I saw a little girl throw a coin in a fountain on a busy Vienna street. She threw it hard and with all her bright young might, reaching back her arm as if trying to match the throw to the gusto of her childhood wish. It skipped across the water and crashed against the fountainhead, then sunk under the stream spouting from an old grey lion, resting with the many other rusting hopes. She sat, and watched the water a moment, then, looking around and recognizing no one, whipped around and sprinted back to her mom and dad as fast as she cold. Her sister and parents had been slowly walking away to give the girl some privacy.

I saw a girl, older than the first but still in the throes of youth, leave behind a wet flower. The young boy she tried to gift it to, presumably her brother, considered the rose much too grimy after she had dipped it into the fountain waters.

I saw an elderly couple, one played candy crush and her partner looked through pictures.

I saw a family of five lick their ice cream and watched the youngest child grow restless after finishing his first. The father and son left in conversation over a shared chocolate cone, and the mother and daughters followed closely.

I saw a friend threaten to throw her companion over the edge and into the splashing and murky water. They both laughed and sat in silence for a while.

I saw a foreign man send a scenic selfie to a friend and peruse his music library for the song to match.

The city glowed amber, and its lamps were like the embers of an ever- fading fire, more resplendent for its finiteness.

And in all these images, I felt the lonesome road for the first time in a long time. Where once my melancholy would stem from one, it was now pervasive, contained in it all. These connections, these moments, these loved ones, were with me, only by happenstance, and this saddened me. The face of the girl in the box saddened me, the face of the girl I had gone on this trip to forget saddened me, but I had no tears left to cry, having left them all in the corner of an apartment lobby under the mailboxes of the people who lived there. I would not have shared them in so public a place anyway.

No, as much as I wanted to, I did not cry in that beautiful place, nor did I remain. Rather, I caught myself scolding my mind for inciting yet another existential crisis in a perfect European square, under glistening lights and the gaze of happy strangers, and pondered over how many more of these I was going to have before I figured out what it was I must be looking for.

I smiled, feeling foolish and a little annoyed, and because somber face certainly did not belong here.

22:15

With renewed zeal for my plan, I found my phone and typed in the recommendation of my hostel roommate.

The Café Mozart was not far from my lionhead fountain.

Inside, I ordered a spritzer because it had gin and sounded classy when I read it. The waitress, who tilted her head at my abrupt shift from German to English, brought a magnificent glass brimming with pink bubbles and a glass of sparkling water, which I usually hated, on the side. For all its price, the drink was not what I had hoped for, and I felt the enthusiasm for the night receding again. Already I had forced fate and been left wanting, and this distasteful 12 euro did not bode well for the remainder of my big-screen experience. After it was nearly empty, however, I forgot the sourness and felt what a joy it was to be drinking where Graham Green even might have.

I settled into my plush booth and watched the vacant tables grow, one by one. The salt shaker danced on the white tablecloth while I grew comfortable with my present circumstances, and by the second drink I was thrilled once more to be here.

22:37

She walked into the café in tow of two friends, the three of them looking as cool as a Woody Allen movie and dressed, again, in what befitted the cozy, elegant lounge.

There go my excuses, I whispered with my head buried in the mule. But how the hell am I going to initiate this? This second drink was drained much quicker than its predecessor because it was something to do in a panic.

22:43

In the end, I didn't have to think about it, because I couldn't. When she caught my stare, she didn't let me go, until I was standing at her table looking all elbows and Adam's apple.

"Guten Abend, uh, hello."

"Who are you?"

"Me?" The six discerning eyes on him made it clear to whom she was referring. "I'm, just, I was at the concert with you tonight. Or, I think it was you? I don't know, I'm sorry." I chuckled, defensively.

"Worüber redet er?"

"My friend wants to know what you're talking about."

"I'd be thrilled to tell her, if I knew."

"Thrilled?"

"Happy."

"Oh." She smiled, understanding, and the friend on either side mirrored her. Maria translated and the three had a short conversation while I stood above them, like a waiter waiting for a decision.

"My friend thinks you should sit down," she abruptly turned back to me.

"What do you think I should do?"

"I think you should do something."

"Fair enough." I whipped my head around for the nearest chair and scrambled for it while they whispered excitedly, and the service staff eyed the odd foreigner suspiciously when they heard the felt padding squeak against their pristine marble floor. I placed the heavy wooden seat and its worn cushion across from the young women, subconsciously supporting the group interview atmosphere perpetuated by their inquisitive gaze.

"What's your name?"

"Sam."

"Yours?"

"Maria.

And this is Sophia, and Ella." The two perked an eyebrow in response, respectively.

"Who are you?"

"Me? I'm just a tourist."

"Just a tourist." Ella listened disapprovingly. "Where are you from?", Maria continued, without the contraction, in the endearing and obvious alliteration of a non-native English speaker.

"I live in Ukraine," I prefaced, softening the blow, "but I'm American."

"You live in Ukraine?"

"As a volunteer."

"You said you were a tourist."

"I am, in this country. But I work there."

"That's rather odd for an American, no?"

"I'm a rather odd person."

Maria leaned her wrists onto the table, and I felt the force of her focused consideration. "Is that why you are here alone?"

"I wanted to come alone."

"And why is that?"

"So I'd be free to talk to you."

Though their comprehension seemed minimal her friends could sense that I had made a leap, in the way I blushed through the words and in the way Maria drew herself closer, further isolating the two of us.

"Are you sure it was only me you wanted to talk to?"

"Of course," I lied, as she expected me to, "why else would I have attended that concert?"

"It was not for the music?"

"That was the icing on the cake."

"I'm sorry?" Ella and Sophia, who had been talking quietly in the background, shared her confusion when she turned around for an explanation.

"Right, sorry, it means like, the music was an added bonus, like, an unexpected benefit of something already good. Like icing on a cake."

"But icing is usually expected on a cake? Isn't that part of the cake?"

I threw my arms up. "One would think. But, you're right. Maybe it's not expected? I don't know, it's just an expression."

"That you use without knowing the meaning."

"I guess. Usually with idioms everyone just assumes they know what you're talking about."

"It is not a very effective way of communicating, then," she teased.

"Oh, it's very lazy. But we Americans have a reputation to uphold."

Maria laughed, in a light and measured manner, and the waiter came with a water and a bill. The girls each ordered a coffee, and I asked for one as well.

"So, Sam, if I am the cake, as you said, how did you know where to find me?"

The espresso was bitter, and I pretended to enjoy it. "I couldn't! It must have been fate."

"Or Google."

The sharp response startled me, and I smiled despite the sour aftertaste on my tongues. Yes, but what are algorithms if not humanity's best guesses at destiny."

"So you believe in destiny?"

"I believe I was meant to be sitting here with you right now."

"Why?"

"Because that's what's happening."

"How do you know you didn't twist it for your own benefit?"

"How could I have? I saw a movie a few months ago, then I decided on a whim to visit the place where it was filmed. After I purchased the tickets, I researched things to do in Vienna, and I bought a ticket for a concert because the hall was magnificent in the pictures and the performance had great reviews. Then, once the concert was over, I went for a drink at a famous café because a famous old-Hollywood movie was written here. And with all these random decisions, on this one night, in a strange city, I've seen the same person twice, and both times felt an overwhelming desire to introduce myself to her. It's a stretch, but it's also quite the coincidence, if nothing else."

She made a small tear in the recycled paper of a sugar packet and deftly split a few grains into her small cup, then emptied it in a single sip without stirring.

"What was the movie?"

"It was this stupid romance."

"*Before...*"

"*Sunrise*! Yes! Have you seen it?"

"Our English teacher made us watch it to study conversations."

"Seems pretty racy for a classroom. Inappropriate."

"Well," she smirked, "us Europeans have a reputation to uphold." Sophia stood up for the water closet.

"Did you like it?"

"What?"

"*Before Sunrise.*"

"Yes, of course, I loved it! It was cute, even if she was French."

Something in her intonation inspired within me an imprudent confidence. Her smile, her effortless beauty, in a very real sense drove me momentarily mad, and though every fiber of my rationality had until this point held the idea as a fantasy, I ventured to her my preposterous plan.

"What are you doing tonight?" I heard my own words like they came from a prerecorded list of options, and my heart, whether with the caffeine and alcohol or the sheer stupidity of what I was going to propose, beat loudly in rapid and rising succession, demanding my full attention. I didn't hear her response and continued as if she had said nothing.

"Because I had this, idea, when I first decided to come here, to do my own Before Sunrise."

Café Mozart danced as the nerves tunneled my vision.

"What do you mean?"

"Well, I only planned to stay for a night, and because it was only one night, I was going to stay awake the whole time and spend every hour I had here awake and exploring the streets. I was going to do this by myself, but I figure there's no harm in asking you to join me, especially because it might be useless and much more difficult to experience this alone."

Her friends stopped and stared at her, apparently enjoying a much less-tentative grasp on the English language than I had given them credit for. Maria drank in theirs and my barely-bated anticipation. "What exactly are you proposing?"

"You and I spend some time here, make sure neither of us is a murderer, then we spend the rest of the night getting to know each other while we walk around Vienna."

"Hm."

She switched to an eagerly-expected Austrian, and Sophia and Ella listened with wide and incredulous eyes, then returned to their conversation confident of my ignorance.

After what felt a painfully long interval which gave me ample time to grasp what I had done and fully realize the ensuing panic, and during which each of the three shot their own attempts at a piercing or mischievous approximation, discernible in any language, they appeared to come to their decision.

Sophia finished her coffee, Ella busied herself with her phone, and Maria said yes.

"On one, condition, however."

I said "Anything" like I was programmed to say this.

"We are not having sex in a park."

With that, I melted into a blushing pool of awkwardness and disbelief. I did not come to until well after I had paid the checks, we said goodbye, and parted ways under the awning, when the brisk evening breeze jolted me back to my unlikely reality.

We stepped out of the closed restaurant, Maria and I, and walked voiceless for some time. The conversation had stalled, once she stopped asking questions and I was alone with her. The people and sights of a nearly vacant and dimmed Vienna were dialogue enough, and both of us needed some time to readjust to reality, as often happens when one sits too long inside, and makes plans for outside, the enchanting atmosphere of a fanciful café, but any silence between strangers loses its charm of contemplation quickly.

Soon, it grew heavy and impenetrable. Looking down at the sidewalk, I thought of everything I might say, but it all terrible. It was too soon to ask about her parents. If she agreed to accompany me, she must not live with them, or they must not be expecting her. If I asked her why she agreed to walk around the city with an imperfect stranger, she would immediately grasp the absurdity of our situation and run for the nearest bus. If I asked her about herself, like how she speaks English, I'll appear shallow, and who wants to spend an entire night answering banal questions.

Then we passed the Viennese Opera House, and all I could think of was that I preferred the architecture of its Lvivian counterpart.

So I said that.

We saw each other in the streetlight for the first time, and the angle of the lamp must have been flattering because she asked me what I meant instead of calling an Uber.

"It's just, the exterior doesn't convey the same expression. It almost feels like the spotlights are doing most of the work, too. Don't get me wrong though, it's still a gorgeous building."

"But compared to another...", she waited.

"Exactly! But what does that say about me, if I see something so beautiful and can't help but compare it to something else?" I actually, inadvertently and later to my serious concern, spoke from a place of real disquiet. I knew that I had in my young life already witnessed much of what would be my most beautiful experiences, be it childhood Christmases when Santa was still alive, the northern lights with a spray of salty ocean, or a dimly lit kitchen host to my mother's baking on a rainy summer day.

Maria sensed my sincerity, and this impression seemed to dispel some of her inhibitions, and with that, the opening lines of our nocturnal relationship were revealed.

"I think that's pretty normal. It's natural for us to judge our present with our past. It's how anyone ever has survived more than a day in the world."

Multisyllabic words rang melodic in her accent's alliteration. "Na-ture-al" flowed smooth and tantalizing, like frozen yogurt from a self-serve machine.

"But does that mean I can only enjoy things in the context of what I've already experienced? Sounds a little limiting, don't you think?"

"Maybe."

"You look like you have more to say", she tilted her head at me, and a lock of her dark brown hair strayed across a softly freckled cheek.

"I guess, like, I know that I am fortunate to have already been guaranteed so many beautiful memories. But if there is nothing singularly wonderful, a moment which stands alone, apart from anything I have already been privy to, what's the point of seeking new experiences? When do we stop experiencing new things for their own sake?"

"Do we ever?"

"As kids we do, right? Each mind is born blank."

"But there's a lot of input before it starts working."

"Those aren't really memories, though. How old are you in your earliest memory?"

"I'm not sure. I don't know the last time someone's asked me that."

"It has to be after you were at least three or four?"

"Do you know your earliest memory?"

"Of course. I was three, and my older brother and I were playing in the yard behind our house, and my mom called us inside, because my little brother had pooped in the bathtub and she couldn't watch us from the window anymore."

She stopped. "How the fuck do you know that?"

I laughed, both at the Austrian version of "fuck" and the reaction I was hoping to elicit with my prompt answer. "Our family had this tradition growing up, on our birthday we always tried to remember our earliest memory."

"Ah. This makes more sense."

"I'm not some weirdo, I promise." She smiled, and started walking again. I mentally kicked myself for saying weirdo.

"But whatever that memory is for you, it's pure. There was nothing informing it when you were in that moment, it just was. And the same goes for most early experiences. Then, at certain point, the mind is full enough to make connections with what's stored there to everything it encounters. I'd like to know why. If it's possible to change that."

"Yeah, me too...

Although", she slapped my shoulder with the back of her hand, "there must be plenty of first times left for us! I have never walked with a tourist all night!"

"There's a first time for everything!", I said, but I wasn't satisfied. "Even now, though, you're still comparing this conversation, me, this weather, this part of the city, with something else, aren't you?"

"Not on purpose."

"I don't want to either! But we have to! That's what makes me sad when I think about it. And confused. Like, why do people still travel if they know in their hearts there's no place like home?"

"What is somewhere else is better than home?"

"It's not about better or worse. It's that they'll always be either. Never so different that it can't be compared."

"You know what they say, though, you never know how good you have it until it's gone."

"Mhmm."

"Maybe that's why people try new things. Not only is it different, but it helps them appreciate what they have."

"I always thought that was kind of lazy. Like saying 'you never know how good it is until it's gone' is something people said when they were too afraid to be present in their lives. Why can't we know how good something is without comparing it to something else?"

"I think maybe you are a weirdo, Sam."

I turned around to face her and walked backwards so I could shrug my shoulders in the most comical way I could. A man in flip flops carrying a large backpack in his hand shouted something that must have been "watch where you're going." I spun around and narrowly avoided him, instantly remembering where I was and my anxiety over maintaining a low profile in every foreign country I couldn't explain myself in.

Maria shouted something back at the passer by, then burst into laughter,

"Definitely a weirdo!" She liked that word.

We crossed a wide street with a trolley track in between two lanes of traffic. The temperature was falling, and the air was misty. With rain threatening again, Maria had us duck into a waiting area. An old woman eyed us curiously before returning to her bony hands and soft whistling.

"Where are we going?"

"You'll see."

No one else joined our shadowed overhang, and its metal bench was cold. The neon sign with the expected arrival times went unchanged. The streetcar didn't come, and wasn't coming, and Maria looked distraught about not knowing her city as well as she expected I might expect her to. I told her not to worry, and that I preferred walking. Especially with the night still dawning. This turn of phrase, in hindsight, was predictably perplexing.

"You know," I explained, "I invited you tonight. You don't have to worry about playing host, because honestly anything we do is better than if I had been alone all night."

This seemed to cheer her. "You would definitely have gotten murdered."

"See, you're saving a life! Don't worry about anything else, you've done your good deed for the day."

We smiled, and we escaped into the moody drizzle. The woman at the bus stop kept waiting.

The scenic route took us along a strip of well-lit watering holes, where young and old milled about, full of vast hope and cheap liquor. At the cusp of this night-life strip, brimming with dawdling opportunities, was an elegant lounge on the first floor of a four star hotel whose décor promised to wipe out my bank account. Walking beside the patio, both envying and criticizing the well-dressed silhouettes, we espied a group of Americans, distinguishable for their loud conversation about the Department of Defense's careers. They were a group of five large and suited men and one woman who was the only one to notice us. Maria stopped us alongside, facing the street and the closed pharmacy across it.

"What's wrong?"

"Nothing," she made as if to shut me up. From behind us, the spurious dialogue continued, disjointed by rich pretension.

"We've loved being here."

"Yes. It's a shame you won't be staying."

"Well, not all of us can have such a posh placement."

"Did you get everything done?"

"Mostly."

"We went back today for the dress."

"Oh yeah, we've been there. Lovely place."

"Did you guys ride, or what?"

"We did the royal cabs yesterday. The driver's English was impossible to understand, though."

"I love listening to these people," Maria interjected on our eavesdropping. "I don't know how it is, but in English you can have the most boring sounding conversations."

"Boring people are boring in any language."

"Yes, but there's something about your countrymen that encourages it. They're usually the culprits. I used to come here, at night, and listen to them. It was easy to practice my English hear, because they are always talking about the same thing, and always loud, and boring. The vocabulary does not vary. I can't imagine how many times this same kind of chat has happened on this patio."

"I guess it comes with the territory."

"Of course. You would never talk about your salary at a bar, would you?"

"There wouldn't be anything to talk about."

She smiled and brought her hand to mine. "You're one of the good ones, then."

Our hands remained tied as we continued forward. Before they would be out of sight, I turned and saw the woman on the patio still watching, but it was too dark to determine what she thought of us.

00:29

A little further down the road was a dive bar, the sort with a heavily graffitied entrance and stairs leading immediately to a basement. The air was heavy, and alive, and a large man with vibrantly tattooed arms, who looked as if his whole life he had been told he would be a bouncer but who also wanted to do it on his own terms, swiped our left hands with a marker.

At the bottom of the stairs was a lobby, to the right a siting area furnished with second hand couches and eclectic picture frames framing inspirational or pensive quotes, and from the hallway heavy dance music overflowed from the club in the back room. The light was low and reflected off the discolored walls of indie album cover collages and personal testimonies written high and low and in innumerable handwritings. The motif was angst.

Maria ordered two drinks, recapturing her easy and moving comfort. I waited alongside her, and followed as she brought us to a loveseat, the legs of which had been scarred by a small and feral dog.

"So how big is your family?", she asked, and handed me a glass of gin with a sprig of thyme hanging on the crystal rim.

"I'm sorry?"

"You mentioned your brother a little while ago. Is he the only one?"

"Oh, no. I have 5." I was happy for this line of questioning, my responses always evoked curiosity, though I had done nothing to earn it. Thank my productive parents for allowing me several minutes of the interest of any stranger.

"What?"

"Yeah," I laughed, always amused by the similar reaction to my sibling count. After a pause, I added, "And one sister", with practice.

"And you are where?"

"The second. And my sister is the youngest of all of us," again, with choreographed certainty of my partners incredulity.

"She is… wow. She must be very happy to have so many older brothers."

Expecting a declaration of her easily-spoiled position in our family, or a hackneyed observation about future boyfriend troubles, her observation struck me.

"Why do you say that?"

"It is obvious, no? I would be very happy to have so many brothers."

"Not always."

"No, always. I am sure of it."

"Do you have any?"

"None. It is just me and my parents."

"I'm always wary of only children," I said, winking above the clinking ice cubes. She looked confused over hers.

So I added, "suspicious."

"Why do you say that?"

I still wasn't sure if she understood. "I'm joking. I've always wondered what it'd be like to be an only child."

"Yes, but you said wary. Why would you be wary?"

"Do you know what it means?"

"Of course."

"I'm kidding."

"Are you?", she scrutinized.

"Well, mostly. But I do think that most of the stronger personalities I encountered growing up, or even now, the kind of people who tend to dominate conversations and who I often let lord over me as a kid, they tended to be only children."

"I understand."

"I'm not saying it's a bad thing!"

"Well yes, we are certainly stronger than most. But I suppose at the same time you think none of us know how to share. Or that we are worse at relating to other people? Or that we are more creative and more isolated?"

"No! Of course not. I'm only saying it's a pattern in my own life, it doesn't apply to everyone."

"This is funny, how you say only like that, and then say only children. Aren't we all just only children?"

I took a sip to buy myself time.

"Mach dir keine Sorgen, mein Freund! Don't worry! I am learning developmental psychology. I love talking about this, nothing you say could offend me. Besides, us only children are stronger, you're right."

While we took path of least resistance into a conversation about her university studies, two young women sauntered from the dance floor to our corner of the bar. I use saunter for their sake, I recall their leisurely pace was more a result of a step by step struggle to stay aloft than a brimming confidence. They landed heavily in chairs to our left and right, and we paused to greet the lolling visitors.

"Hi, who- "

"WERE YOU JUST SPEAKING ENGLISH?"

"Uh, yeah." Maria and I exchanged an amused and annoyed look, the kind reserved for uninvited bar interactions with patrons just drunk enough to be slightly entertaining as well as boisterous.

"WE'RE SCOTTISH! WHERE ARE YOU FROM?"

"SKYE, you're shouting at them!"

"Sorry! We just came from the back"

"Yeah, and we were coming to get drinks, and then-"

"-Then she hit me and was like, I think they're speaking English!"

"And no one could understand us back there"

"Or even at the other bar"

"So we had to come say hi!"

"Because I broke my phone!"

"Yeah she broke her phone, and hers is the one with service so we can't even use Google Translate right now."

"And people keep telling us that they speak English and then when we talk to them they look at us like we're speaking a fucking foreign language!"

The two shared a timeless friendship dynamic, finishing each other's drunken sentences with thoughts of their own and somehow still maintaining a coherent train of thought. It was poetry in motion, yet not the motion of their quipped dialogue but the swaying of their heads while they rolled through a recount of their night's adventures. I could hardly keep up with their slurred accents, and when I looked at Maria it was clear she had lost them a long time ago and was now solely engaged by the dynamic facial expressions of the two Scotswomen. What saved us both was the late arrival of what appeared to be a Chinese funk group, who began setting up their equipment on the nook's the small stage minutes before the friends finished their winding story and would afterwards have awaited our reaction and likely been disappointed by it.

They early tuning notes from what may have been an electric recorder and a metal standing bass drew their attention. Maria smiled at me in that mutual survivor kind of way, put her hand over mine, the squeezed it tightly.

"I remembered my earliest memory! I think!"

"Really!"

"Yes! You talked about being an only child, and then while those two were going on and on and I couldn't understand a word, are you sure that was English?"

"Honestly, I have no idea."

"But then I remembered, I remember sitting on the swing with my grandmother. She was this woman who always wore blue, no matter what, I remember that. And she would always wear these great big blue hats and I remember they looked like the sky floating on top of her cloud of white hair. She was singing to me, this old folky lullaby, and the dog, that's why I remember! We had a dog, a dog that was supposed to be my sibling, I think, and she came to sit next to us, and there was an apricot tree so we must have been in our backyard, I remember from the pictures…"

I squeezed her hand in returned, listening intently until the live music started and the recorder cacophony made any thoughtful interaction impossible. We left quickly after that.

She paid for our unfinished drinks, and we ducked back into the night.

1:45

Our conversation was superficial for a while after.

Then, on a green bridge that spanned a dry canal and crisscrossed with the metro crossing which roared every 15 minutes, I saw a small photo taped to the stud of one of the beams. It was a picture of Ethan Hawke and Julie Delpy, deep in their scripted dialogue on this same walkway. I recalled vaguely from which direction the two Austrian playwrights entered the scene and turned to see if movie history would repeat itself.

The night was lonely, though, and we were not invited to a play we later forgot to attend.

Maria noticed too the picture on the bridge of the bridge, some cinephiles small homage to the film. The light from the streetlight struck the image like a spotlight, and their frozen, smiling faces, alit with the shine of nascent love and the one working bulb overhead brought the image into sharp relief against the darkness of the canal and empty streets and of all the romantic European cities behind. We were held, for no short time, in silence, by this flittering shrine to whimsical yearning and tenderness.

That is, until I interjected with a rash thought.

"You know what always bothered me about that movie?"

"What's that."

"It's just, the whole premise of the story is based on the fact that Ethan Hawke's character- "

"Jesse"

" -Jesse, right, that would've bothered me. Jesse's character isn't supposed to have any money. It's the whole reason he decides to walk around Venice all night in the first place."

"But he doesn't have any. He has to borrow even a bottle of wine."

"Ok, but what about the train car meal? And if he's flying home, he needs money for the bus to the airport, for the car once he's back in the states, all of these things that require at least some money."

"She could have paid for the train meal."

"True, but what about the café they go to later?

"I think she pays for that as well."

"Well regardless, he has some money. Now then how does he come to the dramatic conclusion that his only option is to stay awake all night? There had to be several cheap hotels or hostels in this city, even 15 years ago."

"The same way you did."

"But I chose to do this. He was forced into it."

"Didn't you ever stay up all night with your friends, talking into the morning in a living room on a Saturday night?", Maria asked, her face to the photo, held tight to the structure by two pieces of dirty Scotch.

"Of course."

"And no one was forcing you to stay awake then, no?"

I shook my head.

"What about other nights like that? There must be more," she was right, "and I suspect they were also because you chose not to," and even more sentimental with her memory than I was with mine.

"There are."

"Tell me about one."

"Sleepless nights don't make for good stories."

"This one might."

I stopped.

"For you and I, maybe. But why else would anyone bother to listen to something that has nothing to do with them? The thoughts which keep me awake can only ever be interesting to me."

"Unless you find someone who shares them."

"Have I?"

"I guess there's only one way to know."

"Fine. But you have to tell me why you chose to come with me."

"Well we have all the time in the world, don't we?", she glanced at me in her peripheral above a blushing cheek.

"There is a lot of night left."

"So tell me."

"…"

"There is one. I think it was few months ago at this point. I couldn't sleep, of course. But this, thing, insomnia, it rarely happens to me, and I didn't know how to stop it. The harder I tried, the more frustrated I became. I didn't have anything to do the next morning, but I was trying to fall asleep earlier. I wanted to try and be more productive in the morning. I went to bed before my usual time, and I ended up laying there well past then.

Eventually, I gave up, and pulled out my laptop. But the same show I had been watching before I turned it off to go to sleep, I now had no interest in. I tried reading, but my mind was going a million miles an hour and I found myself rereading the same paragraph and comprehending none of it. I got angry. Like there was some mental block I had formed in my own mind, keeping me from sleep, robbing me of my next day. The longer I was up, the less of my tomorrow I would have. It was irrational, and absurd, but I was angry. After a few minutes of me sitting there, fuming, tossing my book across the room, I finally threw off the blankets, put my jacket on, and went downstairs."

She looped her arm around my waste, both of us watching the wind play with the paper. "Couldn't you have just masturbated?"

The Catholic guilt which sprang at the word got caught in my throat and I nearly choked on it. My coughing echoed down the concrete sides of the channel underneath.

"Is there something wrong with that?"

"Uh, no. I just. It's weird. Never mind. Let's just say that wasn't really an option anymore."

"So you already had masturbated."

"Maybe."

187

I had learned from an early age, in a household of religious adolescents, to never admit to what all knew we were doing, often and everywhere.

She laughed, and the bouncing noise chased my guilty coughs down the waterway. "You're so weird, you know that?"

"If you only knew."

"Ok fine, you weirdo. I won't make you say it." She nestled closer. "You were going downstairs."

"Yeah, I went outside. I was upset, but not at anything or anyone, really at the fact that I wasn't sleeping. I didn't mind that I was going to see the dark windows of other apartments, where I knew everyone else in the city was peacefully dreaming. I just wanted to be outside. Or I needed to be.

Right when I left my apartment, though, one of neighbors came home, probably from a bar, and was stomping up the steps towards me. Halfway to the door at the bottom of the stairs, I knew I'd walk past him, and I knew that in his drunken confidence he'd have a question for me, and I knew I didn't want to talk to anyone, especially not in Ukrainian. So I turned around, and as softly as I could, I scampered back up the stairs. Ran quickly.

But I had to be outside. So I went past my apartment, my neighbor pausing to burp on a landing below, and I ran up to the top floor. I remembered always wondering about how to get on the roof, but this was the first time I had actually made it past my floor, all the way up the stairwell.

There was a door there, and it was unlocked when I tried it."

A booming thunderclap, like the muted clash of cymbals, pealed across a sky suddenly devoid of its stars. We looked down from the invisible clouds and saw the further lights of apartment windows and storefronts glistening behind an encroaching downpour. A current began to form in the canal, and we felt the precursors in our hair.

The picture held steadfast to the storm, but we sprang immediately from our seats and across the rest of the bridge, where there was an awning leaning over a closes pharmacy with a 24 hour window, and perhaps a sleeping attendant behind.

"It never really happens like it does in the movies, does it?", she said, and I wiped rain from my face with a damp shirt.

2:22

"So you never finished your story!"

We were well into the city now, walking astride city park where a solitary biker made laps around an abandoned construction zone, possibly looking for an entrance to reach the Port-o-potty behind the gate. Or that's what I'd have been doing.

"It's stupid." The more I considered the story I had been about to tell her, the more I realized it was hardly that, the more it sounded like a rambling series of non-events culminating in an esoteric epiphany she couldn't appreciate.

"You promised."

"I know, but there's really nothing there. Seriously. I went to the roof, and the wind in the night air was cold, and it calmed me down. That's it."

"I think there's something you're not telling me."

"I wish there was! It's just a bad story, that's all!"

"Something made you think of it."

"I know. And I'd love to tell you what that was, but now that I'm thinking about it, I know I won't be able to communicate what that was. What that open space, under the stars, completely alone, contemplating an unwatched universe, was for me. It inspired something, I spent the rest of the night writing notes in the writing section of my phone. But what that was, or how, or why, I'm just realizing is impossible to share because this is the first time I've tried to."

"Then let me see what you wrote."

"You don't want to."

She stopped us and took her hand from mine to hold it outstretched, its palm expectant. "You're not getting out of this. I'm not going to do something so crazy with someone who wants to stay a stranger."

So I gave her my phone, my notes which had always felt the most deeply personal possession I had to my name, my notes which I never let anyone read but in the case of my sudden demise would make for an accurate, albeit convoluted, summation of who I once was. I let her scroll through these, until she, either on whim or intuition, paused at a particularly revealing folder, and I redirected her to the entry in question. While she read I, in bewilderment for the moments which had led us here, watched her face for any reaction.

After a few nervous minutes, she scrolled to the top of the page, and handed my phone back to me.

"I would love to be a pigeon."

"A pigeon? Why?"

"They live on the rooftops in all the most beautiful places in the world. They can fly to anywhere, and look down on everyone. It's like you said, a city can only be seen from its higher points, just as life can only be understood when you step out of it."

"But any bird could do that. Why would you want to be a sky rat?"

"A sky rat?"

"It's what my friends and I call them."

"Well because of this, exactly. They are like rats only because there are always so many of them. They are invisible in that way. No one pays attention to pigeons. They can go wherever they like, and no one ever stops to ask why. They can sit on the roofs for as long as they please, and if I were a pigeon, I could fly to a church steeple and think about what you wrote for as long as I wanted to. Then in the morning, when the stars were gone, I could fly to the Danube and take long naps on the boats docked there that no one ever uses."

"So you want to be a nocturnal pigeon."

"Yes. That is my dream now. Thanks to your words."

We held each other in a gaze not unlike two players would at a game of poker, waiting for the other to reveal themselves, though their intentions were clear to each other. But there was a couple across the street, sleeping on makeshift beds with two suitcases alongside as if this bright patch of sheltered street were the world's least secure hotel room. I felt a pang in my heart at those for whom what we were doing wasn't some grand adventure, and I couldn't bring myself to kiss her.

Maria must have sensed my inhibitions. "Come on, let's go. I need to see the river."

2:47

A squat city bus stopped in front of us, its shocks hissing awake the dozing man waiting on the bench with us. His flipflops looked a poor choice for the weather; I hoped he was on his way home.

Following him, his white ring of hair the same hue of his collared shirt, we stepped from the soft golden light of the city and into the shocking, cold white fluorescent of its public transport, lighting meant to encourage safety and security but this late at night only highlighting sharp tribalism in the faces of its passengers. I followed Maria across the accordion-like midsection of the double cars, grasping yellow poles and an atmosphere of wariness before we found two empty seats beside each other. I asked her, softly, feeling very self-conscious with the tired eyes on us, how long we were going to stay on. She rested her head on my shoulder and told me not to worry, and for the first time in a long time, really, since I had begun living abroad, I didn't. I didn't care what anyone else on that bus thought of us. I was going to hold her in this hushed space, because that is what she wanted, and that was what I wanted. For an instant, with my hand around her waist, she was a respite from my customary throes of apprehension. She was the only real person in a sea of expressions like projections and so robbed of their power, and from our grey alcove, in the yellow plastic seats and under a white and harsh and ethereal light, we watched impassively a silent collection of Venetians, watched them gather and disperse, with thoughts only for each other and the beauty of our intersection. We were happy couple in the safety of a dark theatre whose feature presentation was a collage of the city's people, the scenes of which changed at each stop.

There was a family of four out touring too late, the matriarch trying unsuccessfully to swipe her city pass on the transport's card reader and the patriarch trying very unsuccessfully to remain inconspicuous while discerning directions. Their children quickly found seats and occupied themselves with phone games.

There was a group of what could only be described as hooligans, a posy of four teenage boys whose dress and demeanor intimidated some and annoyed most of their other onlookers.

There was an entrepreneurial woman with hands full of keys and supplies, coming home from the store after locking up late.

There was a bearded man with one too many buttons of his shirt undone and one too many glances at each of the women he passed on his way to a back seat.

There was an older gentleman with a messenger bag, seated stoically across from us who smiled when we made eye contact.

There was a man who chose to stand in the middle, oblivious or welcome to the eyes which followed his movements as he struggled to remain upright over the cobbled sections of Vienna's byways.

There was a woman drinking from what may have been a water bottle.

There was a girl with purple hair whose crying eyes held a hint of amusement.

There were several others, unnoted for their blank expression or their face in a phone.

There was a little microcosm on this bright bus, teeming with individuals as silent and observant as the patrons in Hopper's Nighthawks, whose bright light spilled flashed longingly onto empty streets in much the same way.

"We're here."

We squeezed through the crowd and back into the night.

3:12

"You know, I live for public transportation."

"Me too." I returned my hand to hers. "Especially at night."

"Yes! It's like, listening to slow jazz. Do you like jazz? It's better when it's dark out. They both are. There is more to focus on at night. And the people who come out when the sun goes down, I love them! When it is this late, they lose all their daytime inhibitions, and they just sit wherever they can. In the day, they never sit next to strangers. But it's late, they're tired, they don't care. It makes for some very interesting pairs next to each other."

"I'm sure that's what they thought about us."

"I hope so," she said, and led us down the hill.

We followed the sidewalk from the bus station into a more residential section of the city, the outskirts typified by unadorned apartment buildings and convenience stores with dated advertisements yet somehow still aligned with the fairy-tale-esque nature of the more trafficked center. She led me down a hell and underneath a bridge, and the fresh air there told me we were near the river.

On the concrete support wall we walked alongside were the tags of several graffiti artists, of little note in the agglomeration. There was one, however, which stood out to both of us for its legible and English words. "The GODS must be crazy", it claimed defiantly in bold black letters highlighted in various shades of blue and lime-green.

We stood underneath the faded phrase where it hung as melancholic as anything one might find in the street-side windows of Vienna's vacant art galleries, awash in that same supplicative light by the gangway's exterior safety lighting.

As often occurs in such places, the two of us lingered in the view, either captivated or pretending to be for an appropriate time before moving on. Before we continued a trite remark, one which in most circumstances wind a rephrasing of the work's title with its most anticipated response, seemed similarly expected. I offered: "They really are crazy."

Maria smirked, and reached for my hand. "They must be."

At the bottom of the hill we veered from the bridge and came to a dead intersection, where the crosswalk's timer echoed down the amber lanes. I surveyed the streets while we crossed, my eyes rising from common throughway signage and pedestrian accommodation to a sight that could not have been more dichotomous.

At once hidden by its ivied fencing, and too drastically tall to ever be concealed was the most Gothic of Gothic cathedrals, buttressed and imposing, the space between adornments deep crevices, great and yellowed brick supporting ghastly holy men who floated on unlit spires, stained glass with muted blackness which spoke of a hollowed interior. It was a castle for a villainous king, a great and mighty fortress dwarfing the almost feudal apartment buildings to its left.

We were close to the river, and Maria pulled me on. "You don't believe that, do you?"

"Believe what?"

"The graffiti."

"Like, in gods? Or their mental state."

"Gods."

"I used to." I looked back at the shadowed structure. "For a long time, I was devoted to one of them. I even considered becoming a priest."

"What happened?"

"I grew up, I guess. And I know it sounds cliché, but I wasn't thinking about this because I wanted to. It was something that made sense, something endowed on me. Then, I left home, and started, or really was forced to start thinking for myself, which led to questions, questions I didn't have the answers for, and questions I didn't think the church scholars had answered. So I dug deeper, into the ideals I had given my entire life to, and the more I examined what I once took for granted the less convinced I was anyone had any idea what they were really talking about. I honestly felt like it was as if every Catholic had at one point blindly agreed to or been taught something, and perpetuated those beliefs without ever examining them critically, without ever doubting what they were claiming, without ever thinking about what was supposed to be the most important aspect of their lives. And that just didn't make any sense to me. So, eventually, it took a few years, but I left."

"Hmmm."

"Why," I asked, worried I had spilt more than the night required.

"It's just sad, you know?"

"What's sad?"

"That people are so divided."

"On religion?"

"For one thing."

We were in a riverside park, and she talked about how she was a Christian, and how she was an aspiring graphic artist, and what it was like to be Christian in an artistic world. She told me how it hard it had been to reveal these beliefs to her friends, about how difficult it was to feel their condescension and disappointment. She lamented on what she saw as a deeply and unnecessarily divided society, how its people had become, or been taught to be so picky about their beliefs it made them intensely personal and resistant to change once they chose which ones to include in their various and yet desperately individual identities.

I felt guilty while we strode alongside the old trees because I knew I was guilty of all of this, whether deeply religious and looking down on those who weren't, or deeply agnostic and looking down on those I used to look up to. I believe I mentioned this to her. Or at least I wanted to.

When the sidewalk met the boardwalk we discussed how stupid and shortsighted it was to view these and other problems of civilization as a pendulum, an idea both of us had been introduced to in our wildly different upbringings. The expression was that in American politics, or Austrian politics, or, more generally, in society as a whole, there existed a great and constant pendulum, like that of a grandfather clock, and at each end of its perpetual motion were the extremes of human experience. This pendulum swung from left to right, from progress to stagnation, from moral to immoral, and no matter how fixed the culture may seem in a given moment, how slow the arc became, in the scope of time infinitum, there would always be a return to where it had once pointed.

This idea, for us, was frustratingly lazy, especially in its summation of humanity's innumerable and variable leanings. Until we arrived at the riverside, we tried for a better metaphor, and gave ideas as to, if it were true, who might have sent this clock in motion, what really made its pendulum move, if there were not a greater pull to its darker side, and whether the arc could be altered or even fixed in a permanent and hopeful direction.

"Besides," I said, "the idea that the liberals will have their chance after the conservatives, and vice versa, that's like trusting the governance of your country to the solution of the laziest parents in existence. Two kids are fighting over the tv, so let's just separate them and give one an hour with it, and then the next one can have the other hour."

"Except that hour is being in charge of one of the most powerful countries on the planet."

"Yeah. Maybe not a perfect example, then," I smiled.

Then we came around a bend and I recognized the boardwalk where a man had written an impromptu or perhaps a rehearsed poem, but something was different. The vista Ethan and Julie's characters had enjoyed was blocked by dinner cruises and passing barges, and the bright sidewalk was still paved and bordered by the beautiful stonework, but it was dimmer, and colder in person.

We were at the water.

3:45

The Danube was far from blue, more a chasm between the refuges of artificial light. I could smell the water, almost taste the scent of fish and algae as the seabirds cried over a midnight meal and the air blew softly between the docks and ticket booths. I could hear the water, the steady rolling of the abandoned tour boats lolling listlessly over little waves that lapped rather than crashed against the manmade riverbanks to which the empty ships were moored. What was revealed between these vessels and by the reflections of the streetlights, however, was more void than answer, the night's current passing unseen underneath a black and unmoving canvas.

It was here at the riverside, a destination, where I saw Vienna.

The opulence of the fairy tale melted into a real city, the glowing setting of a cartoon world supplanted by reality's imperfections, and so too did the dream of creating a perfect dream melt into where and who I was, truly, rather than the story I had crafted for myself long before ever living it.

So here I was, at the culmination of the journey, privy to the last thing I had to see on my long night, and what I felt was disappointment. Not for the experience, but for the experience I had expected it to be. Fantasies always fall short, especially the ones written and directed by other dreamers.

Had it been up to me, I would have remained there, at the water's edge, my tired mind transfixed by the gentle rippling and beside myself in a lack of sleep and prescience. Yet, as there often exists in moments of disillusionment, something real waited underneath the illusion, or behind the proverbial curtain, and just as the city had materialized in all its flawed realness, so too did Maria's hand become sweaty in my own.

She smiled at me, and I knew that in a million dreams I would never have dreamt the scar on her lower lip, the freckles like star patterns on her neck, the speck of green in her eyes. She was the result of infinite possibilities, as was our meeting, as was our existence at the banks of the Danube, and that was enough.

4:05

Another couple surprised us with their footsteps and soft conversation echoing between the river noise, and I wondered aloud as to whether they were doing a Before Sunrise as well. The words broke the trance and Maria, whose energy was fading fast, suggested we sneak aboard the ship next to us.

Climbing the fence was easy enough, and though the adrenaline came with a rush of alertness after we had taken a couple of the white plastic wicker chairs to the corner of the large viewing roof, sleep came quickly for us again in the guise of a swaying boat.

"You know, the fact that neither of them got tired at all during that movie is bullshit," I complained, through a few yawns. "And the way they just teleported around the city? Where are the scenes inside the stuffy busses, or trying to figure out how to read the city map, or choose what café to sit inside,-"

"They fell asleep in the park, didn't they?"

"Oh, right. I guess they did."

5:15

A harsh squawking sent my heart into my throat and I sprang from my nap prepared to dive into the water to avoid being caught trespassing. Upon further and less panicked investigation, it seemed a swan and a pair of ducks had bene engaged in a turf war but had been sent screaming when a fox darted from the bushes to intervene.

"Hey, Maria."

She stirred from her own inescapable exhaustion, her face resting on those two delicate hands. Her forehead bore a red band left by the ring on her pointer finger.

"We should keep going."

"Where?"

"Home."

5:23

There were a pair of city bikes on the rack nearest our ship, and since we were both fighting fatigue and the busses had stopped running, we rented them and pedaled back to the center.

The wind, at 20 km/h, was exactly what we needed, and we laughed and sucked its vitality as we whipped down silent cobblestoned alleys.

When we came upon the main square, soaring around the fountains and empty walkways and street cleaners, and listened to the rumbling of our rubber tires reverberate against those timeless and majestic facades, this was the moment of that night which felt the most like my daydreams. It was everything I had hoped for, the stage of our euphoria timeless and bathed in amber, heightened with the highs of denied sleep and a romance that would always be new, since, as portrayed in the film, it would dissipate with the dawn.

6:00

We circled the square for what felt like hours, each time around noticing more of our setting and each other. There was a tense moment when a garbage can bottomed out and the noise shot like an explosion through our exhilaration, and the worker handling the trash turned his frustration on the joyful tourists, but this passed by the next lap.

"How beautiful is the opera now?", Maria shouted at me when our legs pumped on pure adrenaline and our course had widened to include the opera house and museum district.

"It's the most incredible thing I've ever seen!", I yelled back to her and the closed windows. "You understand!", her face seemed to say, and the buildings resounded with the sentiment, "Don't let the reality of life make you forget about the joy of living it!"

"Hey, hey!"

I opened my eyes.

My back was sore against the wicker chair.

"Get off boat!"

The morning was late enough to make out a man in the early light, standing on the dock and gesturing wildly.

"Off! Off!"

I whipped my head around, but Maria was gone. I scrambled off the boat and scurried into the trees, with my head down and the boat captain raining down verbal Venetian blows while I yawned.

Pausing at a bench to collect myself, when the shouting subsided, I felt a piece of paper in my pocket. I unfolded it, and read in impeccable handwriting:

Sam,

I am sorry I had to leave. We were so close to the morning, but I knew it is easier for both of us. And if I gave you my number, that would ruin the ending, right?

Thank you for a wonderful night.

Love,

Maria

She'd signed her name with a heart.

I looked up at "The gods must be crazy", still as defiant in the dawn.

9:23?

A tattered billboard poster with an image of beautiful young girl eating a cup of yogurt was the last thing I remember seeing before I passed out on the bus back to Budapest, and it filled me with, at last, rationale melancholy.

* * *

Everything and everyone will pass in varying levels of obscurity, no matter how hard we try to hide. And I think that's the point, what gives beauty to the moments before sunrise.

15.

"We are in the habit of imagining our lives to be linear, a long march from birth to death in which we mass our powers, only to surrender them again, all the while slowly losing our youthful beauty. This is a brutal untruth. Life meanders like a path through the woods. We have seasons when we flourish and seasons when the leaves fall from us, revealing our bare bones. Given time, they grow again."

Katherine May

Dear Michelle,

I've described the Ukrainian railways: The Soviet-era decor, the creaking faux-woodwork, the earthy carpet, the sealed windows, the faded curtains which never stay in place, the stifling coal heating, the scents of the closely-encapsulated public, the relief of fresh air escaping beneath the cabin door unsealed by the most recent smoker, the soap-less, hole-in-the-floor lavatories, the communal meals, the mystifying card games, the treacherous bunks, the musty blankets, the snoring coupe-mates, the silence of an extended, downtown station, the soft, wakeful, rarely-apologetic tug of the attendant, the initial stirrings before a ticketed stop, the blinking, exhausted eyes, the instant coffee, the mystical re-encounter with the outside world after braving the steep extended steps: the shared experience. I've shared some of the characters whom I've met in these travels, keeping the most eclectic to myself simply because they evade all descriptive efforts. I could not in a narrative do justice to their individuality, no matter its wordcount. They, and all others, were those with whom the experience was shared. Without them, the journeys would've been unremarkable.

With the lapse in adventure and the innate facelessness of routine, I revisit the trains. I am brought back, because when I leave this country, they will be what I take with me.

Not the intensive, indiscernible hugeness of my daily life, my slowly abating ignorance of my place within it, or the complete comprehension of this country, its people, and my role among them which hovers above me like a settled stormfront, but the minutiae of a crowded cubicle. Where often my experience is measured in enormity, beckoned as I am by the strict constraints on my time in Ukraine to grasp it all, all at once, like a child trying to capture the ocean in a shoreline sandpit, the train car was where I felt intricacy. Where I was forced to consider the water in my hands, not what I had yet to scoop. Locked away, I looked within. Restricted to what is before you, absent cell coverage, charging ports, or a dining car, in thought and in interaction, a train stokes the creative embers, introduces you to yourself through intimate moments with people you surely will never see again, and takes you away from your world. The tracks offer, in return, a few hours of one more readily comprehended.

As an old friend once said, while reflecting on the comfort of insignificance, "hold dear the places that make you feel small." Ukrzaliznytsia has given me my most limited moments. Smallness not felt since dormitory conversations or underneath the stars at Apalachee Regional.

Especially, when the lights go out, and all that remains are the flashing streetlamps and what light creeps from the hallway.

Though my Kindle is backlit and I'm always on the top berth, where I can nestle with a novel as long as I wish without disturbing anyone else in our dim, narrow world, I close my book when the overhead bulbs are extinguished. Though there is magic in the dark, it is nothing next to the yellow-tinted corridor of an overused, overnight train.

I have precious little time to be there, before the heavy breathing beneath me and the stagnant air it circulates overpowers any sense of reflection, or a stranger's dream wakes them with an urge for the toilet. I maneuver quietly, determined to save this space for myself and let the others sleep.

The door is heavy and does not move on my first attempt. After a brief glance at my unmoving bunkmates, I try it again, with a muted grunt. It slides open on ancient hinges, and I breathe a sigh of relief with the fresh air leaking in through the hallway's frames. Next to the sole charging port is a chair which folds out from the wall, and I move the phone which rests on it so I may do the same.

Leaning against the glass, letting the jolting cabin knock my forehead against the frozen pane, I await the streaking scenes. Signs of life are sparse in this vast Ukrainian countryside, little villages dotting the landscape, but I preferred this. The fewer there are, the better I can see myself, watch my reflection float above the empty tracks opposite, larger than the life inside the car, my arms cut off by pink curtains.

When there are lights, they are always warm, and intangibly inviting. Though I'd know what their reality would be if I remembered my own, I imagine each glowing homestand an inn, a place for a weary traveler to put a head. Then, the houses in the hills take on a fantastical shimmer. I'm alone on a dark, wood paneled train and I don't want it to stop, I'm longing for the distance but I'm not ready to go, because there, when the ephemeral realm slows into focus, I'd be lonely, on my own, stepping off the dark, wood paneled train.

A train is the best way to travel. Tracks are much more likely to go past a person's backyard than a highway or a vapor trail. When I see a shirtless man stretching, or a rusted red grill on the second-floor balcony, I know I've caught a glimpse, of a life otherwise unknown.

In our lifetimes, I imagine it's as close as we'll ever come to the personal experience of interstellar travel: a dark microcosm floating through a darker silence, bound forward by an unseen force, passing infinite stars you'll never reach, hurtling towards an unknown destination.

A compartment door rattles; someone inside forgot to slam it shut hard enough so it could latch. My hair is brushed by a curtain which sprang loose from its hook. The corridor twists and rolls.

When I look back, disparate thoughts spring from abandoned industries which lay in graves outside the city.

No longer born towards something, in this train I am protected from something; in my squeaking seat from the haunted scenes we glide through. Moonlight bathes abysmal monuments, crumbling facades tempt my thoughts beyond the glass, beyond my dispelled reflection. Headlights reinforce the decay; my image on the glass is transient. This world will not know me, and I will not know who built it. It cries in the night, it's every structure is overgrown and incomplete, hollow storefronts and spray-painted signs. The cars are lonely too, the streets are empty, the roadsides forgotten. Dead buildings that will outlive me feels a cruelly-cosmic joke.

This train will take me, as well will life.

We do not choose where we get on, only where we want to go. We ride, until it is our stop. Until we are told to get off. We know the destination, after all, but not what happens along the way.

Whether I sleep or I watch, that is up to me.

When I leave this place, what will I come home as? Should I return to my hometown, and find my life on LinkedIn? Should I stay here and flaunt adulthood? Should I go back to school? Should I become an artist?

On a similar train and a similar night, I finished A Portrait of the Artist as a Young Man. When I started the book, I'd hoped for a definitive answer to at least one of those questions. Why I went looking for definition in a James Joyce novel can only be explained by a subconscious desire to self-inflict doubt. Yet, despite those illusory themes, I discovered something uniquely tangible: I shared many, if not all, of the characteristics of the titular, destined, artist.

This, naturally, led me to wonder. In the cabin window, if I saw in myself what was once deemed as the sapling of an artist, does that mean I must grow accordingly? Can I even trust what I saw?

Since we only have this one life, it is impossible to know what we must do with it. And we must do something with it. Mankind's greatest blessing and cruelest curse is that we can live for more than survival, that we might discover a meaning beyond pure procreation. When I watch nature documentaries, I'm glad the story is written that Eve gave Adam the apple. I wouldn't make for a very good animal. I'm a terrible hunter, it's likely I'm even worse at foraging, and I'm far from assertive enough to hold my own in a turf war. If original sin gave us every other profession, at the cost of our mental stability in an unknowable purpose, so be it. I'll take the rarity of life's unfettered joys, with the existential crises in between, over stupefied bliss every time.

Life is beautiful, and utterly unknowable,

Sam

16.

"All of us failed to match our dreams of perfection. So I rate us
on the basis of our splendid failure to do the impossible"

William Faulkner

Dear Michelle,

I began this letter a week ago, on a Saturday morning next to an
opaque French press that embodied my intent to spend the day
writing.

I planned to tell you about the trip to Belgium I took to
celebrate my 24th birthday, a date which marked the official end
to any comparisons I could make of myself to F. Scott Fitzgerald.
He wrote his first novel at the age of 23. The empirical knowledge
that you'll never amount to your hero doesn't make getting old any
easier, and I felt the best way to make my peace with my empty
personal library was to bolter my experiential one. On a cinematic
whim, captured by the beauty of In Bruges, I bought a trip to that
stunningly preserved medieval, mystical city. We've discussed how
I like to plan my vacations around movies, but it wasn't until this
trip that I fully grasped why. The most apparent reason being if a
place is idealistic enough to merit immortality on film, surely it is
somewhere I ought to see for myself. More subliminal, though, is
the desire to live those lives played out on screen. What is
wonderful about art is the chance to know more than one life, and
with movies, those lives are tangible, they exist somewhere outside
the mind. I guess a part of me thinks that because I can see them,
then I can be them. More than the pages of a book, I can place
myself in the exact places where I saw the characters see, and,
perhaps, I'll be able as well to hear what they heard, feel what they

felt, live what they lived. Of course, though I came close in Vienna, reality is more a funhouse mirror, but despite the distinctions I always find something in these trips of what I had hoped to. Whether, contrarily to Before Sunrise, the romance I sought is internalized, or, unlike Schindler's List, the weight of sorrow is only a memory, what I receive is not what I expected, a sliver of what the drama provoked, but always worth the lesser sentiment, because it is real.

Thus, I went to Bruges, in search of meaning, the reconciliation of Colin Farrell. His character found peace and purpose in those ancient alleys and cannels, so I set out for some of the same.

When I arrived, my journey was a beginning fit for Farrell. I imagined him proudly follow me follow in his footsteps as I sprinted through the Viennese airport to catch a connection that had already begun to board, waited for my bags in Brussels that never arrived, spoke terrible French with an attendant and a conductor, both of whom sent me to a different location than the one I'd thought I'd asked for. Accordingly, my bags were misplaced for two days, and I waited in the airport train station for two hours for the cross-country line which I had watched depart from the same platform I had just been directed away from. During this time, sitting with the consideration that maybe a self-challenge to forego foreign cell service and rely on more old-fashioned survival skills might not have been the most prudent considering those sources of old-fashioned directions all expected me to have coverage. The most disheartening response from a stranger is to "check your phone," especially discouraging when common sense would lead even the most casual of its adherents to an awareness that if someone is asking for help, their phone must not be working. Thus, instead of certainty and excitement, I anxiously scanned the arrival times, holding my breath as departing passengers accelerated and any confidence that I was not supposed to be among them plummeted. My eyes were fixed on the digital boards, their numbers slipping from green to red, early to late, and back again, until finally an English speaker who appeared similarly out of depth gave me the train number to look for and boarded with me enroute to Antwerp.

The speed by which we slipped past the dusky Belgian countryside was nearly indecipherable, and a far cry from the European trains I was accustomed to. I remember laughing at the reading light, in disbelief at the absurdly convenient comfort levels of something built in the last decade. After pestering my unsuspecting companions with "Est-ce Bruges?" every time the train slowed, they yelled at me in grateful unison when at last we arrived at my destination. From the station, I was escorted by the throng to the taxi line, where I met an extremely patient Nigerian expat who drove me to several different hostels until I recognized the exterior of my booking.com rental. Had it not been for the jaunty invasion of Manchester United supporters, teeming the quiet streets and filling the squares with crass and belching echoes, I doubt my driver would have been nearly as accommodating. For the first time in all my international travels, the chauffeur was relieved to have an American in the car. Chants of "Glory, Glory Man United" chased away his taillights, and I ducked into a building far too ornate for its $15/night.

That evening, I had an incidentally iconic dinner with two individuals I'd met while dropping off my backpack in our room. Across from me was a Chinese exchange student on vacation from Paris and beside me a freelance Ghanian sports reporter in town for the Europa League match. We ate mussels under the grand eye of the Bruges belfry and shared a beer behind adorned glass and in the low light of a picturesque pub. Everywhere we went, I was in the movie. The existentialist themes beside, everything was how I'd seen it, a city-sized museum whose splendor seemed solely fitted for dreamy contemplation.

The next morning, my birthday, I awoke before dawn and ran to the city center, where I watched the sun's glow beckon the café attendants to set up their patios, the horse-drawn carriage owners to brush their mares, the streetsweepers to wipe away the last traces of the night's revelry, and the bakers to vent their fresh aromas, and listened to the noise of that iconic old-world square rise to a romantic din, while the bells above rang for my new year.

I spent the day with the archetypes of a charming European vacation: the young friends who worked their local breakfast diner together and who gleefully served the assemblage of international visitors who stopped into their happy world for the time it took to make and consume a waffle and a few eggs, all without a break in their elated banter I would never have understood even if my French was fluent, the brusque old women at the cluttered riverside café who served espresso in real China to her few regulars, whose demeanor softened immensely after my poor attempts at her language and my quiet, pensive stay, the clash of generations between an elderly man and the flash photo of a Renaissance painting he took on a flip phone while the most millennial of millennial girls, sporting bright green hair and a Rami Malek t-shirt, looked on with horrified disbelief, the personable waiter saving for a trip to America who recommended the ray fish and sat with me while I ate the unique delicacy and answered her questions about my home, the band of retirees who had spent more nights in this bar than I'd been alive for and played a drunken collection of covers to their own delight and the amusement of the crowd, and the au pair from Atlanta who was working for a family in Brussels and spent the night flirting with a fellow tourist in the hostel bar into the long hours of the night.

It's a birthday I won't soon forget, with memories of windmills and gardens and art and churches and the most scenic coffees I'm ever like to have.

I planned to tell you about it, in the details it deserves. I meant to describe the next morning, the grueling 55 km bike ride I took with a heavy city rental and a few hostel friends through the countryside the coast of Amsterdam, past shipyards and over retrofitted World War 2 bunkers and through cobblestoned lanes and into an unrelenting headwind, not to mention what I saw in Brussels, but, instead, I checked my phone.

This was my writing routine.

Was, because I'll never know a morning quite like those I knew in Uzhhorod.

With the morning traffic lulling me into the daylight, I'd throw open the balcony door, slide into the prerequisite household slippers I'd been gifted by my outraged landlady when she discovered I didn't own my own pair, shuffle into the green-tiled walls of my toilet room, then to the sink in the bathroom, then down the hall and past the several authentically-Eastern European religious icons, the Lord looking forever-disapprovingly at the hour of my waking, into the kitchen, where my breakfast nook hosted the glass of water I never finished and the radio I'd use to keep my Ukrainian sharp, onto the rear-facing balcony, the one that overlooked the courtyard and was reserve refrigerator space in the winter and storage in the summer. I'd wait here, look for my line-of-sight neighbor whom I usually shared eye contact with while he enjoyed one of several cigarettes, and listen to the birds while I waited for the noise of the electric kettle surpass the idle chirping. From this vista I could make out a nearly endless array of apartment buildings identical to my own, with their own courtyards in various levels of use or overgrowth, depending on the number of children who lived above them, and, in the distance, the mountain peaks we shared with Slovakia.

When the water boiled, I'd come inside, grab a breakfast biscuit, and let the oily sludge coagulate until black enough to press, then bring the prizes of my morning foray back into the bedroom, where I'd sit with my coffee and watch nature docs or Comedians in Cars Getting Coffee until inspiration arose from the metal mug I held directly beneath my nose. The day's remaining hours waned quickly once it did. This was my creative process, firmly entrenched and relied upon. Any success I've had in communicating my experiences to you throughout these letters has been beholden to this schedule, whether in the village or the city.

I have not returned to it since, nor tried to write anything for weeks. The long mornings have been unavailable to me since my last one.

The final step, while I waited for the caffeine to take effect, was to scroll through my phone, catching up on texts to kickstart my language functions. On the morning in question, the initially distracting messages, group chats with an unusual number of allusions to a virus, and evacuation, swelled to an absorbing concern, then to a reality, which set upon every comfort I'd so desperately established like a predator on unsuspecting and defenseless prey.

I loved that apartment. Those mornings. That bed, which was really just a couch with an extra blanket folded atop the cushions. I loved the yellow wallpaper, the massive TV stand without a TV, the broken fan, the carpets which never stayed in place, the eternal dust, the window/door with the strange handle system I never truly learned how to operate and often cracked open when I wanted it to swing. I loved the spare room with its entire life of memories I've added to with my abandoned guitar and worn roller bag. The tea sets, the jarred cherries, mildew, the spiders, and the million hangers had a magic I missed out on as a child: we never stayed in one place enough to have a cluttered attic. I loved the creaking floors, the bulbs I had to replace every week, the dry detergent I wasn't able to reach when I spilled it behind the washing machine, the cabinets which never failed to surprise me with their contents, no matter how many times I searched them, the wardrobe and doorframe and all the other creative places I'd found to hang my wet clothes, the table where I hosted Dungeons & Dragons and English clubs and volunteer reunions but that I never drank at by myself.

I loved it all. I loved my life there, and I hate that I'm relying on photos to describe it to you.

I said no goodbyes there, to those whom I was leaving, or to who I was within. I said no goodbyes to the cracked sidewalk which ran alongside the busiest street in the city, the little shop whose "authentic American Hamburgers" I'd been too scared to try, the grocery store where I'd spent nearly all my living stipend since moving to the city and discovering a variety beyond potatoes and instant coffee, the Ukrainian Orthodox church with the blue domes that matched the sky on the most beautiful afternoons, the marshrutka's, the babucyas, the abandoned hotel where I had my first Euro-rave, the candy shop, the shoe-repair place, the building with the lake behind it where I met a dentist who launched one of my more memorable mental crises, the pines I'd slipped underneath on my way to a midnight train, the bus stop I took to Hungary for my weekly youth clubs there. I said no goodbyes. Not any that meant anything. The world, my world, had never truly been mine, and it took little notice of me when I left, disappearing within the 24-hour window I was given to be in the capital.

I wonder, if I'd left on my own terms, whether the goodbyes would have been any different. Whether they would have given me the closure I've longed for since, or whether they would have occurred at all. Leaving in the middle of the night was true to my experience in Ukraine, but not to what I wanted it to be. If I'd had a few more months to reconcile the two, I wonder if I ever would. At least this way I never had to face the answer, though I know in my heart what it would likely be.

The insanity of evacuation was typified in the tears of my site-mate, who was distraught by the tragically few months she'd been able to spend in a place just beginning to become home. For her sake, I kept any remorse at bay during those 16 hours we spent together on our way out. I had had my time. For myself, leaving early was something between, neither fortune, nor misfortune, a fitting end to an incomprehensible time in my life, dense with experience and absent any resolution. This was my time. It was time for me to go.

When we rejoined the others, on our last leg from L'viv into Kyiv, it was starkly evident how alone I was in this acceptance.

Though we made the most of our time, we laughed, we thought, and we cried through the week it took to flee the country, there was an undercurrent, unspoken, expressed in merriment or misery, insisted by smiles or downcast eyes. It was a frenzy, a frantic comprehension of our rapidly changing lives, a bold rebuttal of awareness, a dismissal of a reality we couldn't have wrapped our heads around if we tired. It was as if we all just accepted the absurdity, embraced the chaos. It was either that, or try to make sense of something we'd never understand.

So we drank espresso martinis and kefir. We snuck into each other's rooms after being handed our daily meal, prepackaged and from behind our first of innumerable plastic dividers. We went out at night, to walk around the airport hotel, or to walk the city streets of the downtown one we were moved to after our flight was cancelled for the first time. We spent hours in the airport, initially, a mob of unresolved emotions milling about like locusts in a dead field, picking at whatever was left in the vending machines and the one café still open and unfortunate enough to not be beyond the safety of airport security. We bounced from group to group, wondering what was next, waving at the reporters who'd come to see us off and instead watched us clean out the entire terminal of beer and premade lunch wraps, we gathered publicly in an international airport for the better part of five hours a day for the better part of a week while we waited to escape a pandemic. Some of us wore masks, most of us didn't have the presence of mind to worry about why we were leaving, only that we were.

The strangers thing was that all of this was fun. Pure, mindless, manic, chaotic, and, in certain cases, denialist, fun. Of a kind available only when one is powerless to one's circumstances. Since I grew up, on some indiscriminate date, this week was the closest I've ever come to recovering true youthful abandon. We were like children, ferried from one place to the next, our only consideration the moment, and how we were going to spend the last of our time together. I bought a nerf gun from the toy section of a last-minute souvenir shop and used it to hunt the more depressed among us for a semblance of a cheered expression, I shot caps across the crowd with a friend, I dawned my green fake-Adidas track suit every morning like a Catholic school uniform and went about this manic adult recess because it was the only thing to do.

When at last we were sent back to the hotel, from the airport at the end of another day of fruitless flight-planning as our higher-ups scrambled to get 350 people out of the country while the borders closed and the number of messages from angry parents to overwhelmed Congressmen and women mounted, we were sent home with a snack, an orange or a Snickers bar or something to hold us over until another of our supervisors could corral a dinner, and with a warning to keep our phones on, in case something happened in the night that changed our prospects. It was the largest and longest consolidation of Peace Corps volunteers, one

213

of us even arriving a day late because she had been 20 hours away from her site when the news came in.

Then, a week after that first text and the incessant scrambling of tens of government employees, melancholic moments shared by hundreds of volunteers in a lively limbo, thousands of calls and texts updating love ones already hunkered down across the world, millions of dollars of taxpayer money, and one somber sunset, one bus ride simultaneously the longest and shortest of my life, one four hour security line where I resurrected the infantile atmosphere, this time to protect myself, by offering my colleagues rides around the waiting area with a borrowed luggage cart, and one glance in an airport mirror later, we walked across the cold Kyiv-Boryspil tarmac to the chartered plane that would take us home.

My last Ukrainian sun rose in electronic tint-adjustment windows.

I remember little of the flight, exhaustion and sadness serving to temper any experience to a quiet hum, like the drone of the quadruple engines. When we arrived in Washington it was much of the same we had seen in Kyiv, long lines and trickling information, except for this time we shared the hotel rooms and could order Chick-fil-A on the Uber app. We waited for our connecting flights, saying goodbye to those with more convenient itineraries who stepped out the Hilton doors one by one. The rest of us waited for the call, and watched our fast friends disappear into the world we had all left behind.

I know it was the last time I will see many people with whom I was once inseparable. We will carry each other in our memories of Ukraine, but even these will fade. One day the ones we relied on will be those we used to know, pronouns in an old story.

I don't know how to end this, Michelle.

I wish I could show you all the endings I've written, both before the evacuation, and since.

I always knew I'd say goodbye to this once in a lifetime experience. It's the only way by which a time can become once in a lifetime. It has to end. I think that's why it's been so hard for me to finish this letter, though. Knowing an ending is coming compels you to dwell on what is ending much more than is likely necessary, or healthy. It's why high schoolers can hate their experience of high school until the rose colored glasses are handed out at the beginning of their senior spring semester, why the final bastions of youth are so precious to those soon to lose the last of their vitality, why the saddest death is one which can be marked on a calendar.

So how can I hope to send this off with the conclusion it deserves? The accepting, satisfying ending, the one which brings all the storylines softly to a close is as rare in real life as it is on TV, and was ripped from all of us by this pandemic.

All I can comfortably give you, all that feels authentic enough to transcribe here, is what I wrote down in my notes as we rode from the hotel to the airport late on our last night in the country.

Rather than edit it for readability, I thought you deserved these thoughts in their rawness. Besides, any changes I made were wrong: I'm too far from this moment to know how to capture it in any other way than how it has already been.

I hope it makes some sense to you, as it must have to me at the time.

On the bus from downtown:

I came here to try and see if there were answers abroad.

I soon realized that the language that's on the billboards has very little bearing on the language in my brain. The way in which people greet one another has very little bearing on whether I can overcome a bad habit. So then, I chose, with the vast surplus of time allotted to me, to focus on the dilemma of purpose. If you're anticipating a solution to life's greatest mystery in the next lines, in the next years, I hope you'll still let me come and see you despite your disappointment.

I came to no conclusions, only an acceptance of the chaos.

I experienced, in these two years of self-inflicted isolation, which I brought about hoping I could become someone else, (add something about irony here) myself.

The sum total is what one may call a cosmic joke. Wonderful, in a sense, that the universe might have existed for nigh on infinity and at some point within this endless existence it showed itself, through my own grasping of its irony, the truth of its chaos, and came to love itself through me. How many stars exploded, how many humans lived, how many of my own cells died before I learned this lesson. Before I, heard the joke that's underneath everything.

That entropy is uncontrollable, that change occurs most effectively when we avoid it.

It's a weird, and wonderful thought. Realization, whatever you want to call it, as long as you don't call it a resolution.

Because that's the problem with cosmic jokes: the punchline is always the same: death, nothingness, the inevitability of my insurmountable insignificance. That universal experience and universal ending is the only real resolution.

Thus, I ask myself, if I know the ending, why read the chapters in between?

Have I answered this question by asking it? Is that the answer I came for, that the question which brought me here was what I hoped to find?

My life, however unfortunately, is not a sappy mystery novel with a provocatively-faceless couple on the cover which you can read by the cover.

My life, all life, is possibility. Unknown.

Even the moth that lives for an hour lives for an hour, and for something. The chance to exist.

For me, a perspective by which the universe has never before seen itself, to discover a part of this existence. That's my chance.

It's the same reason I watched the movie you spoiled for me, the same reason anyone eats a Philly cheesesteak, the same reason a terminally ill child still dreams. For the in between.

I came here under false pretenses, and false pretenses are disappointing. And disappearing.

And as suddenly as it started, it was over.

(Please excuse the cliché)

* * *

Consider this, and every word I've sent, my best attempt to fulfill the promise I made to you years ago: that when I came back to the States, when what I left you for was finished, you'd be the first person I visited. Instead, flights are cancelled, and cities are shut down. Instead, all I can give you is this letter, and the knowledge that you are the first person to know what all of this was like. It's a story sure to dominate the rest of my life, and you heard it first. Instead of being there, know, that on my last night in Ukraine, I think the country was aware. When I stepped out onto the 12th-floor balcony of my downtown hotel room, where the whole of old Kyiv was below me, the train station and the McDonald's, where I began and concluded so many of my trips in the distance, after I had just finished a pirated version of the Rise of Skywalker and eager for a few gasps of fresh air before I fell into a restless and premature sleep, I saw a sunset, more piercing than any I've ever felt.

The sun burned through a gap in the twin apartment buildings to the west.

The setting sun is a blazing orange the last time it sets for me here.

The windows of this city are on fire.

Endings really are tricky, aren't they?

Until I live enough to write again,

Sam

Epilogue.

"It seems that the more places I see and experience, the bigger I realize the world to be. The more I become aware of, the more I realize how relatively little I know of it, how many places I still have to go, the more there is to learn. Maybe that's enlightenment enough; to know that there is no final resting place of the mind, no smug clarity. Perhaps wisdom is realizing how small I am, and unwise, and how far I have yet to go."

Anthony Bourdain

Dear Michelle,

A year ago, I addressed a letter to you from the basement of my parent's house in Denver. No longer a volunteer, I no longer needed the abandonment of routine, the long hair, the foreign language, or the abdication of autonomy. Suddenly, I was in a world where these were demanded of me, where the sense of adaptive acceptance I'd cultivated for two years was unwelcome, and out of place. I began my mornings as I had in my own apartment, with a cup of coffee and a soft playlist for a soft mind, absorbing the weather and the scant responsibilities ahead. There was, however, no place for me to run. The things around me were too familiar, and gave my waking mind a sense of structure too rigid for any other self-awareness than the one which was customary for me to feel around my family. I laughed with my siblings, shared the Keurig with my mom and the patio with my dad, all the while feeling far too comfortable. Her questions about what I would do today, or his about what I would do with my life, reminded me I had long left this home, and it was not for me to return satisfied. My childhood, in the sense I could live in the same house as my parents and feel entirely in place there, was over.

I did not admit this with anguish, nor did I accept the impression with delight. Caught in the middle of both circumstances and sentiment, I did the only thing I knew to do.

I sought the unfamiliar.

Since that afternoon, when I called my older brother and began to plan a trip to visit him and his wife in Alaska, a trip only I knew was a one-way ticket, my life has been a tenuous balance between choice and current. I chose to live in their spare bedroom, upstairs as a transplant and disruption, however embraced, in their well-established lives. My brother and I ate big breakfasts and watched Law & Order for most of every morning, while his wife went to one of the only jobs which still required her presence. As a doctor in an out-patient care facility, it was only a matter of time until she brought home the virus which has brought us all together. I did not choose, then, to be quarantined without taste or smell for two weeks, to visit the hospital to monitor heath palpitations, or to be so dramatically faced with my frailty and lack of purpose. I chose to recover, with them and in myself. I chose to finish a novel I'd begun on a lonely day in Ukraine, to hire an editor, and to spend the stipend I was sent back to the States with on Alaskan adventures and freelancers by the word. I did not choose, a month later, to recognize the impression I'd overstayed my invitation. I chose to stop pretending to look for work, and find a place to spend the time I was home alone aside from my desk or bed. I did not decide that the only practical option which was actually hiring to be a Starbucks, I did not choose to be interviewed, nor did I choose to make surprising eye contact with the cute barista with the piercing gaze. I chose, however, to find a thinly-veiled pretext to ask her out, and, over coffee, I chose to misrepresent my knowledge of anime, and whatever other interest she hinted at. I did not choose to give my whole life story, to spill the entire extent of my limbo, or my most developed and passionate opinions. I chose to accompany her to a birthday party, and spend the evening in the car searching for a sign to kiss her. I did not choose to think about the way she watched me spill my soul to a stranger, the way her eyes demanded my full self and attention, the way she penetrated with a question I would be reticent to ask of myself. I chose to call her, I did not choose to talk for hours on end, watching the late summer sun setting while I played in the gravel outside my window. I chose to hike with her, to go thrifting with her, to eat sushi with her, to date her. I did not choose to fall in love.

I chose to relinquish my role as a barista for one as a recovery coach at a youth rehabilitation center tucked into the Alaskan mountains and far away from the civilizations which had let these kids down, abandoning myself to the full sense of absurdity I'd discovered in the writings of Camus while still overseas and enjoying the wealth of spare time which allows for philosophy. I did not choose to fall in love with this job, to encounter stories which I will carry for the rest of my life, and to be guided by these struggling young people to the sense of purpose I'd craved so desperately for so long. I chose to see them as real, to remember my own childhood and encounter them as I would've liked to if I were still a teenager. I did not choose to discover a latent passion, an undercurrent of impetus for youth work that had perpetuated since my mom brought home twins from the hospital and I had ignored since I learned of things like money and fame. I chose to look at ways to make this youth rehabilitation my life, and chose to take the LSAT. I did not choose that the only law school which had a scholarship available to former Peace Corps volunteers was in Philadelphia, nor did I choose my lackluster application, which I typed out to the ticking of the twilight clock on an overnight shift at the facility, while the children slept and I watched to make sure none of them acted on their worst, nocturnal impulses, be accepted, with the financial support I needed to ensure it was the only viable option. I chose to end my year in Alaska, to leave behind loved ones and beloved places and the brutal winter, I did not choose to accidentally apply for the early start and necessitate these goodbyes be sudden and sad, leaving in May instead of in August, and missing out on one more midnight sun summer. I chose a basement sublease I shared with a research student many degrees smarter than myself, I did not choose to later find a perfect second-floor studio, with a window which looked out over the only four single story buildings in the city, giving me a view of downtown I could not otherwise afford.

Since that last night in D.C., the one I told you about, when I laid down alongside the Potomac and reconciled my grief with my reality, from Ukraine, to Alaska, my comfort was the stars. At night, lonely, lost, or listless, I would put my headphones on, play an ambient noise I thought matched their coldness, and seek them out to find comfort in their stillness. Now, my stars are these skyscrapers. I watch their windows from my own, glass that holds a side street and busy sidewalk and which would be an ideal setting for an article or novel that espouses the romance of a bustling metropolis and never quite captures the loneliness of playing witness to infinite lives you will never be a part of. I know this sentiment is surmountable, all I need to do is stand where I look and greet rather than watch. Yet, on nights like these, when I need perspective, I keep my gaze on the shining, empty towers. I keep my gaze on these stars, blocks, which may as well be lightyears, away, and go to bed when all their lights are off.

In this unfamiliar, seemingly vast but ultimately brief in scope, in this year which felt like 10, I understood a simple truth: When you live in change, you'll live the thousand lives you feel your awareness deserves.

Mortality is mitigated by movement.

What I mean is that we are forces of entropy. Our lives are meant to be chaotic, and when we fight this uncertainty, when we abandon confusion for comfort, we lose some of what it means to be alive.

Without discomfort, we can live without temporal awareness, that which plagues those tortured by the insistence of their mortality. Routine, then, is the luxury of forgetting time. But when we have so little of it, why do we seek to be removed from its significance? In discomfort, we fight habit, we reject that which lulls us into indifference, that force by which we are carried 30 miles from our front door before we remember if we locked it, 30 miles we have no recollection of. The same habit which makes front doors disappear, stairs formless, daily motions meaningless, repetitive expenditures of energy imperceptible. Habit that steals the taste of coffee, the sound of conversation, the joy of walking, the softness of a pillow you were once so thrilled to own.

Thus, despite the thousand natural shocks that flesh is heir to, the thousand ways my life has not been what I expected from it, I am happy in the disquiet. Though the idealistic escapism which moved me to apply to the Peace Corps was a far cry from altruism, though the desperation to be unique, to be noticeable, born of my place in a big family or my place in the world beyond, bade me break from the life I'd envisioned, the life envisioned for me, has been a wealth of grief for all involved, though, like Daisy the Great, sometimes all I feel I'm doing is trying to convince myself I'm alive, Ukraine showed me the beauty of existence available only to pain. As such, I am honored to echo the words of Frank Herbert: "I meddled in all the possible futures I could create until, finally, they created me."

I think therefore I am, I am therefore I will die. I will die therefore I must live urgently.

So I went. I said goodbye to you and urgently embarked on this journey of self-discovery, just to discover the more I became aware of myself, the better I understood this self would not always exist. To have found myself only to know I will lose myself seems an ironic tragedy second only to living and never accepting dying. I guess, then, this is what life is. One, great, beautiful tragedy, where we find things, then we lose them, we learn things, then we forget them, we meet people, then never see them again, we live, then we do not.

We are already dead to vast places, untold realities, and countless people. To a still greater number, we will have never lived at all. When I think about those friends I'll never share another second with, relationships wrecked by linear progression, I wonder if I'm still alive to you, whether you believe we'll ever see each other again, and whether we ever will. As a child, we make our peace with a passing of a young crush, we let go of an infatuation without understanding what pursuing it might have meant. Like trimming a spring twig, we let go of an offset choice whose significance is unrealized. This is easier when we are young, as our branches itself is still budding innumerably, and more difficult when our lives become more solidified, the awfully narrow nature of our existence actual and apparent. Yet, if we can let go as a child, surely we can make peace with our little deaths to places, choices, and people that continue throughout our lives. Despite this, I find myself hoping what I know to be true will be undone by happenstance, that, somehow, our branch will grow.

Whether ignorance or denial, I write this letter with a dreadful appreciation for the futility of my foolish refusal to accept that there is no script which will bring us back together.

When we met, I might've looked kindlier on a cinematic fate. Experience has taught me otherwise. I know now my life is not a movie. There is no Act 2 waiting to save me from myself. It is both beautiful and terrible that the unscripted tomorrows may be what I wish them to be, what I need them to be, but, as likely, they will be what I have made them. Nothing more than I was before, the yearning of noble midnight aspirations put to rest at sunrise, the goals and desires and changes I set out to embody set aside for an absent story. I sit here and return to the open balcony from which I have written you so many of these letters, and finally understand, or accept, that I cannot change my story by its setting alone. Inciting this circumstantial change, one which, if I were the hero, would surely lead to the pinnacle plot point of personal growth, has not itself led me to a different path. I am still the Sam I was in Chicago, in Metamora, in Denver, in Tallahassee, in Ukraine, in Alaska, in Philadelphia. And I think that's ok, as long as I can be him, and not of him, as long as I can live, and not live his story.

*   *   *

Myself aside.

Something I've been reflecting on, with some distance, is the lack of characters. I wrote a retelling, not a story. The essential element of others was missing

It was never about me. The character of these cities, towns and villages is comprised of those who inhabit them. I thought, perhaps, I was changing, I was the one who, moved by circumstance and surroundings. This impression was born more of ignorance than selfishness, an aftershock of a transient childhood. As a youth the world cannot help but evolve around you. It is the only way to make sense of it all, the only way to find your place within it. As I moved, then, I considered the variations of my experience extending from within. Until I lived in Ukraine, where the stark reality of the external factors were aggressively poignant in the discomfort they lent me, I never faced the impossible depth of the infinite lives which existed entirely separate from my own. When I moved between States, my mind could work around the unfathomable concept that the places I saw had always been, and would continue, absent my engagement with them. Our common nationality ensured I was in proximate enough of an actuality with them so as to allow me to grasp their distinctness without it destroying the subconscious sense that, somehow, their populations could not be, outside of me. Then, I moved halfway around the world, and discovered, in the full spirit of a self-and-superiority-absorbed Joseph Conrad, here were lives in being as real as any I'd ever encountered, who moved through reality just fine without me there to know them. Had I never volunteered, these people and their places would never have known me, nor I, them. It sounds like a natural, morning-coffee conclusion. But for a boy whose world was always shifting, who seized the only commonality and clung to his consciousness as a terrified sailor clings to the stout, intrepid mast in a maelstrom, to know my life was but one of an infinite progression of existences, indistinguishable but from within, to contemplate sonder, was at once being thrown into the churning waters and being able to breath underneath them.

This sentiment, strengthened, I hesitate to tell you, by the love I've since found for someone else, someone who confirms the paltry reach of my insight everyday by upending the expectations I have for our relationship, has dominated my reflection on my service, and these letters. I think, now, I began writing them because I needed somewhere to keep my thoughts while I grappled with the thought that everyone I encountered had thoughts innumerable of their own. They were always, therefore, going to be exercises in introspection, while the events of my greater experience occupied my more waking mind. It wasn't until I was brought outside myself by a deeper desire to connect, that I took up the true effect of what my time overseas had had upon me. Whether by conscious object, or happenstance motivated by an upending, underlying love, until you do the work of desperately seeking a reality outside your own, and face the terrifying limits of your understanding, until you choose, or are forced, to divest yourself of the impositions we place on others to understand them without knowing them, it is impossible to know just how narrow our perspective truly is. In her, and outside of the stories I have shared with you, I finally understand what I love so much about this quote from the beloved song-writer John Darnielle: "The errand of life is to be able to understand as many perspectives as you can." In Ukraine, I stumbled upon this truth: that living for others is the best way to know yourself.

Consider, then, these simple headlines, odes to those behind the words, the reality behind my narratives, the definite people who made my memories what they are. I've said before, the problem with letters is that no one writes them with you. Absent a mature, active understanding of the truth of being, or a second opinion, a second consciousness distinct from your own, dragging you outside yourself and reminding you of the inexhaustive scope of all that is real outside your reality, it is so easy to lose them, and, in writing a memoir, to dispose with the external that a coherent inner history may form. This will always be only the surface of the whole story. If I could rewrite them all, I'd start here.

I'd start with Nina, and her notebook. How we spent each evening, sharing a lovingly-prepared meal and few words from her handwritten English I could never decipher and me from the language lessons she found ample fault with. How she would scold me when I left my shoes in my room. How we would go shopping together and meet all her friends at the market, and I'd sheepishly laugh while the women proclaimed how cute I was and tried to remember if any of their granddaughters were single, and how on our way home, arms laden with fresh produce packaged in old water bottles that had seen more lives than they would have anywhere else in the world, we would take a detour to an old walnut tree, standing in the middle of a nondescript courtyard not far from our own, and would collect whatever had fallen since the week before, and make baklava with the spoils of our urban forage. How, babucya or grandmother, aged generosity is universal.

She made sandwiches for me to take after we said goodbye. I remember eating them while the other volunteers and I milled about a central-Ukraine gas station while we waited for our bus to Kyiv from our training city to fix its flat. From the country's capitol we would disperse, like tendrils of nascent neural connections, all reporting back to the headquarters where we were headed that day. After I finished the lunch she packed for me, I would have a new home, a new host family, and new meals. I would never see Nina again. Though we spoke on the phone as my Ukrainian improved, and though I helped her niece practice English a few times over Skype, I realized all too late that she never cared where I came from. The distance between us was a self-inflicted one. It was never about the language for her. She was simply happy to make me sandwiches, and see me smile.

That last time I saw her, she gave me sandwiches. No one else on the bus had been given a lunch for the road. Simple, and final was this act of kindness. For me, it is her legacy, bread and cheese and processed meat.

Either age or COVID or the war has taken her from this world. Yet, for a time, brief in both our lives, we made each other smile. Over potato pancakes heaped to an impossible height for a quick breakfast, over homemade kefir and little bits of jasmine tea and poundcake, we shared words, incapable of sentences, but communicating more than what is shared by most. She would fall asleep in the kitchen while watching Russian soap operas on her tiny television, and I would fall asleep to the white noise of the talk radio she kept playing to ensure strangers would know someone was home. Or, perhaps, to fight the widow's silence. There, in that apartment, if I ever felt outside of everything I knew, those carpets on the walls, the smell of a thousand loads of laundry and the dirt from the balcony garden, the warmth of the cluttered living room

I never used and the hallway lined with pickle jars I'd creep down to pinch an extra hard-boiled egg if I'd stayed up too late watching movies on my phone, in the space between our rooms where we would each, every night, wish each other a good night in our respective languages, formed in their entirety a place of comfort, an abundant softness, a home.

I'd start with Yarina, my service counterpart, my closest and only friend for a substantial part of my time in the village and, therefore, young life, whom I met while she was smoking on the patio outside a now-destroyed conference hotel. She recognized me before I knew her, the docket of information she'd been given about me had included my passport photo. Eager to introduce herself to the individual she'd advocated to bring in from overseas for nearly a year, filing endless paperwork and surviving the indiscriminate scrutiny of the Peace Corps site-selection process, she hugged me, and immediately posted a selfie of us on that front porch. I will always cherish that image, which exploded onto the local Facebook pages of my soon-to-be community and gave the entire population something to talk about and an unfounded anticipation. I'd tell you about the first meal we shared, in a brightly lit cafeteria over plates with too much dill, the blind date feeling pervasive in the large room, where hundreds of volunteers were meeting their own supervisor/supporters for the first time, two years looming largely, giving undue weight to every mispronounced word and poorly-formed sentence. I'd tell you about the train ride where I watched her smoke a cigarette over the car coupling, how she gave me the top bunk and woke me up when the Carpathians first came into view. How her and I navigated the tumultuous year that was my time with the local council, from an ill-advised introductory presentation, to our attendance at the many trainings and even more espresso, to our stolen, humorous glances while the mayor voiced his weekly displeasures to the entire staff at the Monday morning meeting, to our shared love of a tiny cafeteria which served the best pickled carrot salad, to my time spent babysitting her wonderful daughter in the tiny corner office where I was meant to be productive, to the Christmas carols we sang while we cooked what we could of a Thanksgiving dinner, to those we sang throughout the village in exchange for cognac and cookies, to the visits to her family store and home attached behind, to her connections I met with who ranged from the town's ski instructor to the town's unofficial realtor to the town's de-facto international importer, to the bus rides and markets and apartment visits and to every aspect of my life which she navigated me through. With plenty to be pessimistic about, given the end result of our collaboration and the ignominious ousting from my place and position in our small society, what I have to fondly recall about my work in Perechyn is due mostly to her. She welcomed me without reservation, with a smile she kept for me always, even when our efforts were called into such contentious question. She was a mother when I needed her to be, a colleague when I needed her to be, a guide when I needed her to be, a translator when I needed her to be, and a friend always.

I'd start with the English clubs, the faces of smiling children or young adults that were my weekly respite from the monotony of unspecified office work. In the village, I met with grade schoolers on Wednesday afternoons, in the library across from the mayor's restaurant. I would bring candy, or cookies, or juice, they would bring friends and family members, and we'd spend an hour or two in a unstructured conversation, with games and movies and the goings-on in their young lives more than filling the time. In the spring we took pictures under cherry blossom trees, in the summer, we went to the river, or played volleyball behind the school on the hill, in the fall, we had a Halloween party, we went apple picking on the side of the road, and bought sweaters from the local second-hand store, in the winter, we huddled around the table and watched Eurovision entries on a projector I'd borrow from the town's hotel. Some weeks I wondered what they saw me as, whether a teacher or friend, especially on those days when most of the vocabulary involved gripes with various authority figures or online gaming chats.

With my college English club, this was less a question. In as much as I was there every Tuesday evening, after a scenic 30 minute bus-ride through an impossible-preserved quaint foothill countryside, in the common area on the fourth floor of a university dormitory, speaking in slow but unchanged lexicon, I was also there to spend time with peers, to share ideas for my service, and to meet those who I would spend the most time with, especially after I was transferred to the city permanently. In that largely-unchanging group I found the spirit I'd sought since my arrival in the country. They were passionate to learn, to teach, to work together and to embrace the possibilities of youth, to help make their home the place they knew it could be, 20 linguistics majors who now sew camouflage nets and craft Molotov cocktails to be shipped to the front lines. I'd tell you how they introduced me to Coca-Cola cold brews, showed me the best cafes and reading spots within the wonderfully picturesque places of Uzhhorod, how they laughed with me, played soccer with me, invited me to parties and movies and cultural events and city festivals, how they were my first authentic Ukrainian friendships, and how inspired I was to know them.

I'd start on an exhaustive list of all the other host country nationals I was so fortunate to encounter, from landladies to grocery clerks to neighbors to coworkers to servers to teachers to bus drivers to security guards to pond poets to chess masters to native-Hungarians to summer camp campers and counselors to the taxi driver who drove me to the train which was to evacuate me from the place I'd finally grown into.

I'd start with the other volunteers, the roles we shared, whether friend or advocate or colleague or co-presenter or guide or lover or ex or therapist or patient, the indescribable bond of loneliness and isolation which made our reunions so tumultuous and unforgettable. I'd start, and end, likely, with them.

A year removed from these people, I know they are whose stories demanded to be told. I'd love to go back and write them into existence for you, but the further from them, the more their memories rely on an unreliable nostalgia, the more their complete picture I'd wish to convey is obscured; with the passing hour they slip further from my present. I only hope that to some of them, I'm still alive, or may one day be alive again.

I'd start with you, and bear in mind these letters were never about me. They were my chance to give you that sense of understanding I now seek from the person I love. I am sorry I understood that in hindsight, and that I never got to where you needed me to be. I'm sorry to have fulfilled my promise to write without giving you what you so deservedly wished to read.

Starting with you, I'd go back and re-read your letters. I'd realize, after all, why, despite everything I told you, you continued to ask about me. In all my words, I kept trying to define the experience, to summarize my stories in a way that would make them more conducive to narration, to render my life chapterlike. Instead of telling you about me, I told you stories of me. Well and good, and a glimpse into my world, but never who I was. By the time I had reflected on those moments enough to conceptualize them in a letter, I was entirely removed from their reality. To immortalize a story is to remove both the burden and the importance of its moral.

A few nights ago, I read what you were telling me.

I see what it is you were desperate I hear. That the mistake I made with us, a mistake patterned in my past, was thinking that our story was written, that the typecast was set, that our chapter was over, that the conclusion I'd given us was a natural one. When I left I told myself our history and built our story from the conclusion, conforming memory to the choice I'd made, scapegoating circumstance for the ending I'd created. When I left I made you a character, because characters are at the mercy of their stories. They do not weep at the fate of the final page because their book is written, their story complete. If you were anything else, the consequences of the finale I'd made for us would've lingered longer than I wished to consider them.

This is my story. When my external world changes, I take this to mean what I left behind is set to be written down. Set in stone. That these lives are separate, seen from the light of a reflective author, who knows the past is immovable, enough to be captured on a page.

What an idiot.

Life is worth living because everyone would write your eulogy differently. My existence to the lives of the people I've encountered is not contingent on a shared reality. When I said goodbye to you,

you remained as vibrant an individual as you always were, before, during, and after our time together. That it took two years and a novel's worth of introspection for me to realize this would be embarrassing if it weren't so fundamental. Instead, it's just important. It's just for me to, as you put it, learn, not regret.

And so I'd start by telling you how sorry I am that I never came to see you. It is still a plan I harbor, and another dream I worry I cannot make true. I'd tell you what it was like to pack a bag with a ticket I didn't have a return for, to set my mind against the idea of returning to what I knew until I knew what I was returning for, to tell my parents I'd be gone from their basement for a few weeks, and not seeing them until half a year and half a lifetime later, when I brought the girl I'd met home for Christmas. I'd struggle to encapsulate all I've felt in the past year, all I've felt since that move, since circling the Anchorage airport with forlorn video game music in perfect sync with the scene below, the thawing mudflats which reminded me of lungs, and the perpetually snow-capped peaks beyond. I'd tell you how exciting it was to see my brother and his wife, to eat their vegetarian chili, and to go to bed under a midnight sun. I'd tell you how, when this novelty wore off, as it was certain to, now that I could speak the same language as the gas station attendant, and recognized all the products in her aisles, how difficult it was to readjust to a life that did not demand my ever-vigilant attention, how easy it was to get lost in the days when circumstances did not necessitate otherwise, how I stopped paying attention to my interactions with others when the stopped be a constant exercise in confidence, in adaptation, in learning, in desperation to communicate well enough to be understood. I was in Alaska, but it was still my home country, and no amount of lifestyle differences or scenic unfamiliarity can impose a significance on daily functions as does a billboard written in a foreign language.

I'd tell you all of this, and I'd wonder how an autobiographical memoir is ever possible, when, even in my young life, I find it impossible to define even the parts of my life I've lived since you were in my rear-view mirror. I'd imagine it'd be easiest to start with a title, and think of what would be most conducive to my personal epochs. Certainly, the tale of the lost child caught in the middle of a post-soviet microcosm, the story of fired volunteer, finding love in a tundra place, the apartment by the highway where my life became my own, all seem worth jumping-off points. But, where, then, would I include my thoughts about New Year's Eve, and how every December 31st seems to fall into the category of experiences you're eager to redo as soon as they are over, how sometimes we make so much of things that we allow only for disappointment, and when it inevitably follows, it feels worse than it should? When would I write that when the stories we tell ourselves aren't the stories we live, the difference can be destructive? When would I ask you, or any reader, then, whether you would rather die knowing you had experienced everything there is to experience, or leave at least something to those last moments of your imagination?

Considering, I guess I'm grateful to finally understand my life is not a novel. As much as it flies in the face of who I'd love to see myself as, I hope it never will be. If I could write my memoirs it would mean I could no longer affect my memories, that I have succumbed to my past as it stands, relinquishing any control over the aspects of it that remain alive. It will mean I can no longer change, at least how I might, or could, according to these distinct periods. They will have an ending, and if I write about my time in the Peace Corps myself in Ukraine will become a caricature, one whose influence upon my present has been exhausted. Yet, I know if I nurture them, the lessons I learned while I was abroad will stay with me for a lifetime, and ought to.

Life, my life, is not a novel, because the story changes with everything you see, every touch and taste and scent and sound and person, everything changes, so long as your pages aren't complete.

I'd end, if I were to write it all again, with something like the following.

When you are lost, you are boundless.

When the setting is familiar, you feel its loss. "Do you really want to leave home so far behind?", familiarity asks, each time you leave.

I'd tell you, in the last letter, that for what it's worth, I find myself missing those walks through places I didn't understand. It was so much easier to be aimless there.

I miss you, Michelle, I miss aimlessness, and the million other lives I might've lived. What comforts me is what is unwritten.

Sincerely,

Sam